THE WATCHMAN

Mastering the Ancient Blueprint of Intercession

DR. JOHNATHAN STIDHAM

Kingdom Publications
kingdompublications.com

The Watchman: Mastering the Ancient Blueprint of Intercession

Published by Kingdom Publications
kingdompublications.com

ISBN: 979-8-9957753-0-0

First Edition

Printed in the United States of America

Table of Contents

INTRODUCTION

Answering the Call of the Ancient Guardian

Something has been stirring in you. You've felt it for a while now. Maybe it shows up at two in the morning when you can't sleep and your heart is heavy with a burden you didn't ask for. Maybe it's that sharp sense in your spirit when something is wrong in your church before anyone else has a clue. Maybe it's the way you can't walk past a broken situation without feeling the pull to pray. That's not just personality. That's not just sensitivity. That's a call.

God is raising up a generation of watchmen in this hour. Not casual pray-ers. Not people who fold their hands on Sunday and forget about it by Monday. He's looking for men and women who will stand in the gap between heaven and earth and refuse to move until things shift. The prophet Ezekiel records God's own words in chapter 22, verse 30: "I sought for a man among them who would make a wall and stand in the gap before me on behalf of the land, so that I should not destroy it." And then God says something that should shake every one of us. He says He found none.

That verse is not just history. It's a warning for right now.

We are closer to the return of Christ than we've ever been, and the enemy knows it. He's working overtime to keep believers distracted, discouraged, and disconnected from the place of prayer. The dangerous thing isn't just that people aren't praying. The dangerous thing is that many people who feel called to intercession don't fully understand what they're called to. They pray hard. They pray often. But without knowing the weight of the office they carry, they can spend years crying out without ever stepping into the full authority God designed for them.

That changes right here.

This book is built on one central truth: prayer is not passive. It's not a wishful conversation you send up and hope something happens. Prayer, at its highest level, is legislative. It's governmental. It's the act of a watchman who has studied the laws of heaven, built a case before the courts of God, and issued decrees that the enemy is legally required to obey. When Moses stood before God and pleaded for Israel after God declared He would destroy them, the Bible says God relented. That wasn't Moses getting lucky. That was an intercessor who understood his position and used it. What the enemy wanted to happen did not happen because one man refused to move from his place of prayer.

That is the *Shamar* anointing.

The word *Shamar* is one of two Hebrew words that form the foundation of what it means to be a watchman. It means to keep, to guard, to protect, to watch over. It's the same word

God used when He told Adam to "keep" the garden in Genesis 2:15. It's the word used when the Levites were told to guard the instruments of the tabernacle. It carries the image of someone who has taken responsibility. Not because someone told them to once, but because they understand the value of what they're protecting. A *Shamar* watchman doesn't guard out of obligation. They guard because they love what's on the other side of that wall.

The second word is *Tsaphah*. Where *Shamar* is about guarding what's already in your care, *Tsaphah* is about seeing what's coming before it arrives. *Tsaphah* means to look out, to peer into the distance, to scan the horizon. It's the posture of a watchman who climbs to the highest point and looks as far as their eyes can reach. Together, *Shamar* and *Tsaphah* give you the full picture of what this call looks like. You guard what God has given you, and you see what's approaching before it ever reaches the gate.

Think about what a guard does at a gate. He doesn't wander. He's fixed. He's alert. He knows what belongs inside and what doesn't. When something unauthorized tries to get through, he doesn't shrug and wave it in. He sounds the alarm. That's what you're being called to do in the spirit. You're not just praying for yourself and your situation. You're standing at the gate of your family, your church, your city, and you're keeping watch over what God has placed in your care.

Imagine a woman named Daria, a 38-year-old mother of three who has felt the pull to pray since she was a teenager. She spends time in prayer every morning. She loves God deeply. But for years she's felt like something is missing. Her prayers feel like they go up and bounce back. She prays for her children but still watches them struggle. She prays for her church but still sees division creep in through the back door. She isn't doing anything wrong. The issue isn't her heart. The issue is that no one ever taught her that she carries an office, not just a desire. No one told her that her prayers could become decrees, that she could stand before the courts of heaven and build a case, that she could govern the spiritual atmosphere over her home the same way a guard governs a gate. The moment Daria understands that she's a *Shamar* watchman, everything about how she prays begins to shift.

That's what this book is for.

You need to understand something about prayer that most believers never get taught. Everything that happens in the earth can be changed through the power of prayer, except for what God has already declared permanent in His Word. The return of Jesus is permanent. The final judgment is permanent. But the circumstances your family is walking through right now? Those aren't permanent. The spiritual pressure on your city? That can change. The attack on your church? That can be turned back. The enemy has no legal right to anything that a watchman has covered in prayer and decree. The problem is that too many people don't know they have that kind of authority, so they never use it.

God isn't looking for perfect people to stand on the wall. He's looking for willing ones. He's looking for people who will say, "I'm not moving from this place of prayer. There are too many souls on the line." That's the spirit of Nehemiah, who built the walls of Jerusalem with one hand and fought the enemy with the other. He never came down off that wall. Not when Sanballat came to discourage him. Not when Tobiah came to mock him and slander his name. Not when the spirit of confusion tried to make him forget his assignment. He stayed. He built. He prayed. And the wall went up.

You're going to learn how to do the same thing in your sphere of influence.

What You Will Master in These Pages

This book is going to take you through a specific, step-by-step understanding of what the watchman's call looks like in practical terms. Not theory. Not vague spiritual concepts that sound good but leave you wondering what to actually do on Monday morning. Real, applicable truth that you can pick up and use in your prayer life starting today.

The first thing you're going to understand is your *metron*. That's the Greek word for your sphere of spiritual influence. Every watchman has one. For some, it's your household. For others, it's your local church, your workplace, or your city. Your *metron* is the territory God has given you relational authority over in the spirit. You can't just walk into someone else's territory and start making decrees. Authority in the spirit comes through relationship and assignment. When Paul came to Jerusalem, he recognized James as the apostolic authority of that city, even though Paul carried a global calling. He honored the *metron* of the man who was assigned there. That kind of wisdom is what keeps a watchman effective and protected.

Once you know your *metron*, you're going to learn how to use the Nehemiah Intercession Roadmap to track the souls inside it. Nehemiah didn't just build walls randomly. He rebuilt them in a specific order, and each gate he rebuilt represents a stage in the spiritual development of every person in your sphere. The Sheep Gate is salvation. The Fish Gate is discipleship. The Old Gate is maturity. The Valley Gate is the season of hardship that delivers you from what shouldn't be in you. The Dung Gate is where you drop off everything God pulled out during the valley. The Fountain Gate is where you receive fresh vision and purpose. The Water Gate is the rebirthing of your assignment. Each person in your life is somewhere in that cycle, and your job as a watchman is to pray them through it, not around it.

Most people who need intercession are stuck somewhere between the Valley Gate and the Dung Gate. They've gone through pain but they haven't let go of what the pain was supposed to remove. They're still carrying what God was trying to free them from. Without a watchman praying them through, people can stay stuck in that valley for years. The prodigal son ended up in the pigpen because he couldn't get past the dung. Proper intercession is what moves people through the cycle and into the fullness of their purpose.

You're also going to learn about legislative prayer. This is where everything shifts. Most believers are familiar with petition prayer, asking God for things. But the highest form of prayer isn't a request. It's a decree. It's a judicial act. The enemy doesn't fight through warfare alone. He fights through legislation. He puts people in places of governmental authority who pass laws and edicts that bind entire generations. Principalities, powers, and rulers of darkness don't just wander around causing trouble. They operate through spiritual legislation, through decrees and assignments issued from demonic thrones. That's why when the devil wants to attack your children, he doesn't just show up at your front door. He goes to Capitol Hill and writes a law.

The answer isn't to fight flesh and blood. The answer is to become legislative in the spirit. When Jesus said in Matthew 16:19, "Whatever you bind on earth shall be bound in heaven, and whatever you loose on earth shall be loosed in heaven," those words "bind" and "loose" are contractual terms. They're legal language. When you bind something in the spirit, you're making a spiritual contract that the enemy cannot break. When you loose something, it cannot be bound. You're not just praying. You're issuing edicts in the courts of heaven that have legal standing in the spirit realm.

In Luke 22:31-32, Jesus tells Simon that Satan has demanded a trial against him. The word "asked" in that passage literally means to demand a legal proceeding. Satan was standing before the throne of God, using Simon's failures as evidence to gain a legal right to destroy him. And what did Jesus do? He didn't just say a prayer. He made a righteous decree. He declared Simon righteous, innocent, and forgiven on the basis of the cross. That's legislative prayer. That's what you're going to learn to do on behalf of the people in your *metron*.

You'll also learn how to approach the courts of heaven the right way. You don't walk into that courtroom on the basis of your own goodness or your years of fasting. You walk in through the blood of Jesus Christ. His righteousness is your standing. His merit is your case. When you approach from that place, you can begin to make righteous judgments, bind and loose with accuracy, and issue decrees that shift the atmosphere over everything God has assigned to you.

And then there's the glory cloud. Watchmen don't pray for atmospheres. They carry them. They create them. The Samaritan woman at the well in John 4 is one of the most powerful examples of this. She came to Jesus broken, with a lifestyle that had defined her for years. When she encountered the living water, the Word Himself, her mind was washed. Her desires changed. She didn't want what she used to want. And when she went back into her city, the atmosphere she carried was so different that people who used to follow her for all the wrong reasons now followed her straight to Jesus. She had created a cloud. Everywhere she went, people encountered what she carried.

That's what you're going to build. A life so saturated with the presence of God that when you walk into a room, the atmosphere shifts before you say a word.

The Roadmap to Spiritual Authority

Everything in this book builds toward one goal: making you an effective, positioned, and spiritually authoritative watchman over what God has placed in your hands. The roadmap to getting there runs through specific Hebrew and Greek concepts, specific scriptural patterns, and specific spiritual disciplines that work together to form the full *Shamar* anointing.

You're going to go deep into the Hebrew definitions of *Shamar* and *Tsaphah*, not just as vocabulary words but as offices. You're going to understand why there are different kinds of prophets, and why a *Shamar* watchman is a specific type of prophetic calling that doesn't require you to stand on a platform or preach to thousands. Some prophets see. Some hear. Some write. Some are simply guardians. They keep and protect the ordinances of God. That's the watchman. And you don't have to hold a title or a position in a church for this call to be real on your life.

You're going to study the three spirits that will fight you the moment you say yes to standing on the wall. The first is the spirit of Sanballat, which comes to discourage you. It whispers that you've been praying too long and nothing is changing. It asks why you're still showing up when you can't see any results. The second is the spirit of Tobiah, which comes to slander and mock. It attacks your character and tries to discredit you so that the people in your *metron* can't receive what God has placed in you. The third is the Ashtodite spirit, which brings confusion. It clouds your mind so that you can't think straight about your assignment, your identity, or your calling. All three of these spirits have one goal: to get you off the wall. Nehemiah faced all three and never came down. By the time you finish this book, you'll know how to face them and stay in your place.

You're also going to learn how to build the glory cloud through specific acts of worship. There are Hebrew words for praise and worship that carry distinct meanings and distinct functions. *Barak* means to bow and kneel in submission before God. *Yada* means to lift your hands and confess His sovereignty. *Todah* means to lift your hands in thanksgiving and admiration. *Shabach* means to shout and proclaim His testimony out loud. *Halal* means to celebrate Him with everything you have, the way David danced before the ark with no concern for what it looked like. *Zamar* means to sing and make music before Him. *Tehillah* means to sing back to God what He's putting in your heart. Each of these is a tool. Each one builds the atmosphere around your life. The more the Word of God is inside you, the more what comes out of you builds a cloud that repels darkness and draws people into the presence of God.

Elijah understood this. On Mount Carmel, while the prophets of Baal were cutting themselves and getting no response, Elijah did something that looked strange to everyone watching. He poured water on the altar. He wasn't praying for fire. He was building an atmosphere. He was creating the conditions for what God was about to do. When fire fell and hit that water-soaked altar, the water evaporated and rose into the atmosphere. And when water enters the atmosphere, it forms a cloud. Elijah then sent his servant seven times to look for the cloud he had already created through his act of faith and worship. On the seventh trip, the servant came back and said he saw a cloud the size of a man's hand rising from the sea. Elijah said run, because the atmosphere I've already built is about to bring the rain.

That's the picture of a *Shamar* watchman. You don't wait for the breakthrough to show up and then celebrate. You create the atmosphere of breakthrough through your worship, your decrees, and your consistent place of prayer. And then you watch what God does with what you've built.

The courts of heaven are real. The books are open. Daniel 7:10 describes the scene: a river of fire flowing from God's presence, millions of angels attending Him, and the court in session with the books opened. This isn't poetry. This is the governmental reality of heaven that you have access to through the blood of Jesus. Every time you pray with purpose and authority, you're not just talking into the air. You're entering a courtroom. And in that courtroom, the enemy can bring charges, but you have an Advocate who has already made the decree that you are righteous, innocent, and forgiven.

Your job is to learn how to plead your case from that place. Not from pride. Not from your track record of fasting or your years of ministry. From the righteousness of Christ alone. When you approach the courts of heaven through His blood, you can begin to see clearly, judge accurately, and decree with authority that shifts things in the natural world.

You were born for this. The Bible says God wrote a book about you before you took your first breath. The desires He put in your heart since you were young weren't accidents. They were part of the assignment. When you pray, you can remind God of those promises. You can build a case from what He already declared over your life. That's not arrogance. That's a watchman who knows their authority and uses it on behalf of the people and the territory they've been called to guard.

The *Shamar* anointing isn't a special gift reserved for a few elite believers. It's an office available to every Spirit-filled follower of Christ who is willing to take their place on the wall and stay there. The world around you is waiting for someone to stand in the gap. Your family needs a watchman. Your church needs one. Your city needs one. And God has been looking at you for a long time, knowing that you're the one He wants to raise up for this hour.

The wall doesn't build itself. Pick up your tools.

Activation & Reflection

---

1. What first stirred your heart toward intercession? Describe the moment or season God began awakening the watchman within you.

____

____

____

____

2. What specific territories — family, church, community, workplace — do you believe God has assigned you to guard through prayer?

____

____

____

____

3. What has been your greatest obstacle to maintaining a consistent, Spirit-led prayer life?

____

____

____

____

4. How do you sense God inviting you to grow as a watchman through this book?

____
____
____
____

5. Write a brief declaration committing yourself to your post. What are you willing to lay down to fully answer this call?

____
____
____
____

A Watchman's Consecration

Father, I answer Your ancient call today. I consecrate myself as a watchman on the wall, yielding my eyes, ears, and voice to Your purposes. Open my spiritual senses and teach me the blueprints of intercession that move heaven and shake the earth. I take my post. I will not be silent. Use me, Lord, for Your glory. In Jesus' name, Amen.

CHAPTER 1

The Dual Mandate: Shamar and Tsaphah

Defining the Hebrew Watchman

There's a call on your life that's older than you know. It didn't start when you first felt the urge to pray through the night. It didn't begin the moment you sensed something was wrong in your church before anyone else said a word. That call goes back to the ancient writings, to the language of heaven itself, to two Hebrew words that carry more weight than most believers ever get to understand. Those two words are *Shamar* and *Tsaphah*. Together, they form the foundation of what it means to be a true watchman for God.

Most people who feel drawn to intercession know something is different about them. They feel things others don't feel. They wake up at 3 a.m. with a burden they can't explain. They sense danger in spiritual atmospheres before it shows up in the natural. But without understanding what that call actually is, many of them spend years praying hard without ever stepping fully into the office God designed for them. That's where these two words change everything.

Let's start with *Shamar*.

In the original Hebrew, *Shamar* means to keep, to guard, to protect, to watch over, and to preserve. It's the word used in Genesis 2:15 when God told Adam to "keep" the garden. The same word shows up in Numbers 3:8 when the Levites were told to "keep" the instruments of the tabernacle. It's used in Psalm 121:4, which says that God "neither slumbers nor sleeps" as He watches over Israel. *Shamar* carries the idea of someone standing at their post, not because they were told to once, but because they've taken on the responsibility as their own. A *Shamar* watchman doesn't guard something out of obligation. They guard it because they understand the value of what they're protecting.

Think about what a guard does at a gate. He doesn't wander around looking at the scenery. He's fixed. He's alert. He knows what belongs inside and what doesn't. When something tries to get through that gate without authorization, he doesn't shrug and let it pass. He sounds the alarm. That's exactly what *Shamar* looks like in the spirit. You're not just praying for yourself. You're standing at the gate of your family, your church, your city, and you're keeping watch over what God has placed in your care.

This is where many intercessors miss it. They understand prayer, but they don't understand guardianship. Prayer can be spontaneous, personal, and driven by what you feel in the moment. Guardianship is different. It's positional. It means you've accepted responsibility for something beyond yourself. A *Shamar* watchman prays with authority because they know they've been assigned to a specific territory. They're not just talking to God about things they've noticed. They're standing in the gap for what God has entrusted to them.

Now consider what happens when no one takes that position.

When there's no *Shamar* watchman over a home, the enemy doesn't announce himself. He slips in quietly, through offense between spouses, through confusion in the minds of children, through financial pressure that never seems to let up. When there's no watchman over a local church, division creeps in through small disagreements that should've been prayed through before they ever became public arguments. The damage that happens in unguarded places isn't always loud. A lot of it is slow, subtle, and consistent. And by the time people notice it, the root has already gone deep. *Shamar* is the call to prevent that. To stand before the breach happens, not after.

Now let's look at the second word: *Tsaphah*.

Tsaphah is translated in several ways in the Hebrew scriptures. It means to look out, to peer into the distance, to scan the horizon. It's the posture of a watchman who climbs to the highest point of the wall and looks out as far as they can see. In the ancient world, a city's survival often depended on one person doing one thing: getting to high ground and looking out. If that person was distracted, asleep, or simply not there, the city could be taken by surprise. The watchman on the tower wasn't just an extra set of eyes. They were the city's first line of defense.

That's what *Tsaphah* is in the spirit. It's the ability to see from a higher vantage point than what the natural world gives you. It's climbing above the noise, above the emotion, above the chaos of everyday life, and looking out from heaven's perspective to see what's coming before it arrives. Not every intercessor operates this way naturally, but every watchman must learn to develop this capacity. Because guarding what you have today isn't enough if you can't see what's heading toward you tomorrow.

You don't have to be a prophet to be a watchman. But a certain type of prophetic calling is built entirely around the *Shamar* function. There are prophets who see visions. There are prophets who hear words. There are prophets who write. And then there are prophets who are simply guardians. Their entire assignment is to keep and protect the ordinances of God, the holiness of a house, the purity of a vision. They don't necessarily stand on platforms. They stand on walls. And their prayers are what keep the gates of a church, a family, or a city from being breached by the enemy.

God told Ezekiel in chapter 22, verse 30, "I sought for a man among them who would make a wall and stand in the gap before me on behalf of the land." God was looking for a

Shamar watchman. Someone who would take their place between heaven and earth and hold the line. And the most sobering part of that passage is what God said next: He found none. That wasn't just a problem for Israel in Ezekiel's day. It's a warning for right now. We're approaching the return of Christ, and the enemy knows it. The last thing he wants is a generation of believers who understand their authority and take their place on the wall.

That's why you're reading this.

Imagine a man named Marcus, a 41-year-old who has been in church his whole life. He prays regularly. He serves faithfully. But for years he's watched things fall apart around him, his marriage going through seasons of tension he couldn't explain, his teenage son pulling away from God, his church going through a painful split. Marcus isn't a bad man. He loves God. But no one ever sat down with him and told him that he carries a specific office. No one explained that his sensitivity to spiritual things wasn't just a personality trait. It was a call. The moment Marcus understands that he's a *Shamar* watchman, his prayer life doesn't just get more frequent. It gets more positioned. He stops praying from a place of reaction and starts praying from a place of assignment. And things around him begin to change, not because he prayed harder, but because he finally understood where to stand.

That's the power of understanding these two words. *Shamar* and *Tsaphah* aren't just vocabulary. They're an identity. They're an office. And when you step into that office with full understanding, the way you pray, the way you see, and the way you carry yourself in the spirit will never be the same.

The Genesis of Guardianship

The call to guard didn't start in the New Testament. It didn't begin with the early church or with the prophets of Israel. It goes all the way back to the very first chapter of human history. In Genesis 2:15, the Bible says, "The Lord God took the man and put him in the Garden of Eden to tend and keep it." That word "keep" is *Shamar*. Before Adam ever named an animal, before Eve was formed, before any of the drama of the fall, God gave man one foundational assignment: guard what I've given you.

This is important. God didn't place Adam in the garden just to enjoy it. He placed him there to be responsible for it. To protect it. To watch over it. And tied directly to that assignment was the command to take dominion and expand the garden's boundaries. Dominion and guardianship weren't separate things in God's original design. They were the same thing. You can't expand what you won't protect. You can't grow what you won't guard. The moment Adam failed to keep the garden, the moment he didn't stand in his place as a *Shamar* watchman, the enemy walked right in through the gate.

That's not just a story about Adam and Eve. That's a picture of what happens in every unguarded space.

The serpent didn't storm into the garden with an army. He slipped in quietly, found the woman alone, and started a conversation. He didn't attack with force. He infiltrated with subtlety. And Adam, who was supposed to be keeping the garden, wasn't keeping anything. He was standing right there when the serpent spoke to Eve, and he said nothing. He didn't sound the alarm. He didn't stand in his place. He let the enemy get through the gate and then followed right behind him into disobedience. The fall of man wasn't just a moral failure. It was a failure of guardianship.

God's response to what happened in the garden is revealing. He didn't ask Eve first. He went looking for Adam. "Where are you?" That question wasn't about geography. God knew exactly where Adam was hiding. It was a question about assignment. "You were supposed to be at your post. Where are you?" That same question echoes through every generation of believers who've been called to stand on the wall and walked away from it instead.

Then comes Genesis 4:9, and the question shifts. After Cain kills Abel, God asks Cain, "Where is your brother?" And Cain answers with words that reveal everything about what a watchman is supposed to be. He says, "Am I my brother's keeper?" In Hebrew, that word "keeper" is *Shamar*. Cain's answer was meant to be dismissive, a way of saying, "That's not my job." But God's response to the question is implied in the weight of it. Of course you are. Of course you're your brother's *Shamar*.

Watchmen don't just protect visions. They protect people. That's one of the most important things you need to understand about this call. You don't become a watchman just so you can guard a ministry or a church building or a theological position. You become a watchman because you can't stand watching the enemy take advantage of people. You carry a burden for them. You feel it when they're in danger. You can't sleep when they're in a valley. That burden isn't a burden you chose. It was placed on you. And it's the mark of a true *Shamar* watchman.

The connection between guardianship and dominion runs through the entire Bible. When God gave man the garden, He didn't just say keep it. He said tend it and keep it, cultivate it and guard it. Both things together. Growth and protection. Expansion and security. A watchman who only guards and never cultivates becomes stagnant. And a believer who only grows without guarding becomes vulnerable. God's design was always both. You grow what's in your care, and you guard it from what tries to take it.

This principle shows up in the life of Nehemiah in one of the most vivid pictures in all of scripture. Nehemiah was called to rebuild the walls of Jerusalem, walls that had been broken down and left in ruin. When he arrived and surveyed the damage, he didn't just see rubble. He saw a city without protection. A city where the enemy could walk in from any direction without resistance. And he understood that until those walls were up, everything inside the city was exposed.

So he built. And as he built, the enemy came. Three spirits showed up to pull him off the wall. The first was Sanballat, who came with discouragement. "Why are you doing this? It's pointless. Look how long this has been broken. You'll never finish." That spirit is still working today. It comes to every watchman who's been praying for a long time without seeing visible results. It whispers that you're wasting your time, that nothing is changing, that you should just stop. The second spirit was Tobiah, who came with mockery and slander. He attacked Nehemiah's character, spread lies about him, tried to make people doubt who he was so they couldn't receive from what he carried. That spirit goes after the credibility of watchmen because if it can discredit you, it can cut off the people in your sphere from the anointing you carry. The third was the Ashtodite spirit, a spirit of confusion. It clouds your thinking so that you can't remember your assignment, can't trust what God told you, and can't hold on to the clarity of your calling.

All three of these spirits have one goal: get you off the wall. Nehemiah never came down. He built with one hand and fought with the other. He stayed at his post. And the wall went up.

The *Shamar* mandate from Genesis is still in effect. God is still looking for people who will take their place as guardians over what He's entrusted to them. Your family is a garden. Your church is a garden. The vision God has given you is a garden. And your assignment is the same one Adam was given at the very beginning: tend it and keep it. Cultivate it and guard it. Don't let the enemy slip through the gate while you're standing right there doing nothing.

The original call to guardianship was given before sin entered the world. That means it wasn't a response to the fall. It was part of God's original design for humanity. You were made to be a guardian. It's not something you have to work yourself up to. It's something you were built for. The question isn't whether you have the call. The question is whether you'll take your place in it.

Tsaphah: The Watchtower Perspective

Habakkuk 2:1 is one of the most clear and direct descriptions of what a watchman actually does in the spirit. The prophet writes, "I will stand at my watch and station myself on the ramparts. I will look to see what he will say to me, and what answer I am to give to this complaint." Read that slowly. He says he will stand at his watch. He says he will station himself. He says he will look. And he says he will wait to see what God says. That's *Tsaphah* in its purest form. It's intentional. It's positional. And it requires patience.

The word *Tsaphah* means to tower, to peer, or to see from a distance. It's the posture of climbing to the highest point available to you and looking out as far as your eyes can reach. In a natural watchtower, the person at the top isn't looking at what's inside the city. They're looking at what's coming from the outside, from the horizon, from the direction the enemy might approach. They're watching for movement before it becomes a threat. That's the intercessory function of *Tsaphah.* You're not just responding to what's already happened. You're positioning yourself to see what's coming so you can respond before it arrives.

This is why intercession requires what could be called a "tower perspective." You have to climb above the noise of the natural world to see from heaven's vantage point. When you're standing at ground level, all you can see is what's right in front of you. The argument in your marriage. The struggle in your child's life. The tension in your church. But when you climb to the watchtower through prayer and waiting on God, you start to see things differently. You see the root behind the argument. You see the spiritual pressure behind your child's struggle. You see the enemy's strategy behind the tension in your church. And when you can see it clearly, you can pray with precision instead of just praying out of panic.

Waiting is a weapon most believers underestimate.

Habakkuk didn't just climb the tower and start shouting. He climbed the tower and waited. He positioned himself and then watched to see what God would say. That kind of waiting isn't passive. It's one of the most active things a watchman can do. It requires discipline to sit in silence when everything in you wants to keep talking. It requires trust to stop filling the room with your own words long enough to hear what heaven is saying. And it requires humility to accept that the perspective you need isn't the one you already have. You have to go up to get it.

In the ancient world, watchmen who left their towers were considered traitors. Not cowards. Traitors. Because they knew what they were responsible for, and they chose to abandon it. The city could fall because of one person leaving their post. That's the weight of the *Tsaphah* call. When watchmen are off their towers, the enemy moves in the dark without anyone sounding the alarm. Division enters a church without anyone seeing it coming. Spiritual pressure builds over a family without anyone identifying the source. The damage doesn't happen because the enemy is so powerful. It happens because no one was watching.

The *Tsaphah* function is also about interpretation. It's not enough to see something in the spirit. You have to be able to understand what you're seeing and know what to do with it. Watchmen allow what's in the spirit to manifest in the natural, and they can interpret it. That's a critical distinction. Many Spirit-filled believers have spiritual experiences they don't know what to do with. They see things in dreams or feel things in prayer but don't have a framework for understanding what God is communicating. The *Tsaphah* watchman develops that framework over time through consistent time in the tower, through study of the Word, and through relationship with the Holy Spirit who is the ultimate interpreter of all things.

Think about the picture of Israel going into battle. There was always a person stationed in the tower whose only job was to watch the horizon. Not to fight. Not to strategize. Just to watch and sound the alarm if the enemy was approaching. That person's faithfulness to their post determined whether the army was caught off guard or whether they were ready. One person. One post. The difference between preparation and catastrophe.

You are that person for the people in your sphere of influence. Your family doesn't know what's coming at them from the spirit realm. Your church members can't always see the spiritual pressure building around them. But you can, if you're in your tower. If you're positioned. If you're watching. And when you see it, your job is to sound the alarm through prayer, through intercession, through decree, so that what the enemy planned as a surprise attack becomes something that's already been prayed through before it ever arrives.

Shamar and *Tsaphah* work together in a rhythm that every watchman needs to understand. *Shamar* keeps you grounded in your assignment. It anchors you to what you're responsible for right now, the people and the vision in your care. *Tsaphah* lifts your eyes above the immediate to see what's coming. One without the other creates an incomplete watchman. If you only guard without looking up, you'll be reactive, always dealing with what already got through the gate. If you only look without guarding, you'll see things but never have the authority to do anything about them because you haven't taken responsibility for the territory. You need both. The guard who stands at the gate and the watchman who stands in the tower are the same person. That's you.

There's a practical reality to climbing the tower that nobody talks about enough. It costs you something. Habakkuk said he would station himself and wait. That means he had to stop doing other things. He had to be intentional about getting to the high place. In your life, that looks like carving out time where you're not just petitioning God with a list of needs but sitting in His presence long enough to hear what He's saying about the territory He's assigned to you. It looks like silent listening prayer, where you bring your spirit into alignment with heaven and you wait. Not for five minutes. Long enough to actually hear something.

The *Tsaphah* perspective also changes how you interpret what you see in the natural world. When you've been in the tower and you've seen something in the spirit, you start to recognize its shadow in the natural before it fully manifests. A conversation that seems small but carries the spirit of division. A pattern of behavior in someone you love that signals a spiritual attack building underneath the surface. A shift in the atmosphere of your church that tells you something is off before anyone can name it. That kind of spiritual perception isn't weird. It's the fruit of consistent time in the watchtower. The more you practice it, the sharper it gets.

And when you see something from the tower, you don't panic. You pray. You decree. You build the case in the courts of heaven before the enemy's plan ever reaches the gate. That's the full picture of the *Tsaphah* watchman. Not someone who sees trouble and gets afraid. Someone who sees it coming and gets positioned.

Putting It Into Practice

You now have the two pillars of the watchman's call. *Shamar* is your identity as a guardian. *Tsaphah* is your function as a seer. Together, they define what it means to carry the *Shamar* anointing over your family, your church, and your city. But identity without action stays theoretical. So here's what this looks like when you actually put it to work this week.

The first thing you need to do is identify your post. Sit down with a blank piece of paper and write out the specific territory God has assigned to you right now. Not what you wish you were responsible for. Not the city-wide assignment you're believing for someday. The actual people and the actual vision in your life right now that God has given you relational authority over. Your spouse. Your children. Your local church. The small group you lead. The coworker you've been praying for. Write them down by name. These are the people you are called to *Shamar*. This is your post. You don't leave it. You don't abandon it because you're tired or because you haven't seen results yet. You stay.

Once you have your list, take each name and ask yourself one honest question: have I been actively standing guard over this person, or have I been reacting to whatever the enemy has already done? There's a big difference between a watchman who prays before the breach and one who only prays after the damage is done. The goal of this exercise is to shift you from reactive to proactive. You're not waiting for the crisis to show up before you pray. You're praying now, while things look fine, because that's what keeps them fine.

The second thing you need to do is set a specific time this week to climb the tower. Not a prayer time where you're talking the whole time. A listening time. Pick a day, pick a specific hour, and protect it. Tell your family you're unavailable. Put your phone in another room. Sit before God in silence and bring your spirit into alignment with His. Then ask Him one specific question about your assigned territory: "What do you want me to see about the people you've given me to guard?" Then wait. Write down whatever comes. It may be a scripture. It may be an impression. It may be a name that surfaces in your mind. Don't dismiss it. Write it down and pray into it.

The third thing is to practice sounding the alarm before it becomes a crisis. When you see something in the spirit, when you feel something is off about a person in your sphere, when a dream or an impression gives you a warning, don't sit on it. Pray into it immediately. Decree the opposite of what the enemy is trying to do. If you sense confusion coming against someone you love, decree clarity and peace over their mind. If you feel the spirit of division moving toward your church, pray unity and love over every relationship in that house. You're not waiting for the problem to show up. You're issuing a spiritual decree that closes the gate before the enemy gets through it.

These three steps, identifying your post, climbing the tower in listening prayer, and sounding the alarm through decree before the crisis, are the basic rhythm of the *Shamar* and *Tsaphah* call. They're not complicated. But they require consistency. A watchman who shows up to the wall once a week isn't really a watchman. This is a daily posture. A daily choice to stand in your place and keep your eyes on the horizon.

The enemy's greatest advantage over an unguarded family or church isn't his power. It's the absence of someone standing in the gap. Ezekiel 22:30 says God looked for a man to stand in the wall and found none. That's not the story of your family. That's not the story of your church. Not anymore. You know your call now. You know your words. You know your post. Stand in it.

Activation & Reflection

---

1. In your own words, what is the difference between Shamar (to guard and keep) and Tsaphah (to watch from a tower)? How does each apply to your daily prayer life?

____

____

____

____

2. What specific walls — relationships, ministries, or spheres of influence — has God assigned you to protect through Shamar intercession?

____

____

____

____

3. From your watchtower position, what spiritual threats do you currently see approaching your territory?

____

____

____

____

4. In what areas of your life have you neglected your watchman post? What has been the consequence?

____

____

____

____

5. What practical changes will you make this week to fulfill your dual mandate more faithfully?

____

____

____

____

The Watchman's Prayer

Lord, I stand in my dual calling today. I commit to Shamar — guarding what You have entrusted to me — and to Tsaphah — watching with prophetic eyes for what is approaching. Give me discernment to know the difference between human threats and spiritual warfare. I will guard my post and report to You faithfully. Strengthen me for this sacred assignment. In Jesus' name, Amen.

CHAPTER 2

The Nehemiah Intercession Roadmap

Rebuilding the Pattern of a Believer

Nehemiah wasn't a prophet. He wasn't a priest. He was a cupbearer to a king, a man with a broken heart over a broken city, and a God-given assignment to rebuild what had fallen. But what he built wasn't just a wall. God used the rebuilding of Jerusalem's gates as a prophetic blueprint, a map that traces the spiritual development of every human soul from the moment of salvation all the way through to divine purpose. When you understand this map, you stop praying in circles. You stop praying generic prayers that feel sincere but don't move anything. You start praying with precision, pushing the people in your sphere of influence from one gate to the next, until they reach the fullness of what God designed them for.

That's the Nehemiah Intercession Roadmap. And it changes everything about how you intercede.

The core idea is simple. Every person you're called to pray for is currently located at a specific gate in their spiritual development. Just like the gates of Jerusalem were rebuilt in a specific order, the soul moves through a specific cycle in God. It doesn't skip stages. It doesn't jump from salvation straight to purpose. There's a process, and that process has a map. Your job as a watchman isn't to pray vague, hopeful prayers over people and wait to see what happens. Your job is to locate where each person is in the cycle and pray them forward, specifically and deliberately, to their next gate.

Nehemiah 3 gives us this map in detail. As Nehemiah rebuilds each gate, he's not just doing construction work. He's laying out God's blueprint for the journey of a soul. The Sheep Gate. The Fish Gate. The Old Gate. The Valley Gate. The Dung Gate. The Fountain Gate. The Water Gate. The Horse Gate. The East Gate. The Inspection Gate. Each one represents a distinct stage in what God does in a person's life. And once you see it, you can't unsee it. You'll start looking at every person in your life and asking the same question: which gate are they at right now?

Before we walk through each gate, you need to understand one foundational truth about this roadmap. People do not move through this cycle on their own. There's not a single person walking in their God-given destiny who got there without someone praying them through. Not one. The Bible says the prayers of a righteous person accomplish much. That word "accomplish" carries the idea of force, of movement, of pushing something forward. Your prayers are not passive observations. They're the force that moves people through the gates. Without intercession, people get stuck. They circle the same valley for years. They sit at the dung gate and can't let go. They never enter the refreshing of the Fountain Gate or the purpose of the Water Gate. Proper intercession is what breaks the stagnation and pushes them forward.

Think about the prodigal son. He went through a valley. He ended up in the worst possible place, rolled around with pigs in the mud, in a place of absolute spiritual and natural poverty. That's the dung gate experience. But the story says he "came to himself." Something shifted in him. He remembered who he was and whose he was, and he got up and went home. Now imagine that someone had been praying for that son the entire time he was away. Imagine a watchman standing in the gap, decreeing that the son would come to himself, that the spirit of confusion would break off his mind, that the father's love would become irresistible to him. That's not just a nice thought. That's the mechanics of intercession. The prodigal son came home. But how many prodigals are still in the pigpen right now because no one is standing in the gap for them?

Your prayers are the difference between someone staying stuck and someone coming home.

Now here's something that will sharpen how you use this roadmap. When God began to show this pattern to those who carry the watchman's call, one of the first things He said was this: show me where they're at. That's the prayer of a targeted intercessor. Not "God bless everyone I know," but "God, show me exactly where this person is in the cycle so I know how to pray." When you ask that question and wait for the answer, the Holy Spirit will begin to give you specific insight about the people in your sphere. He'll show you that your brother isn't just struggling. He's stuck between the Valley Gate and the Dung Gate. He went through pain but he's still carrying what the pain was supposed to remove. He's having a pity party in the pigpen and he can't get out on his own. Now you know how to pray. Now you can push him forward with precision.

This is also a cycle, not a one-time progression. A person can go through all the gates and then find themselves back at the beginning of a new season, going through a new valley, receiving a new filling, stepping into a new level of purpose. The cycle repeats at deeper levels as God takes each person further into maturity and destiny. So don't be discouraged when you see someone who seems to be going backward. They may not be going backward at all. They may be entering a new revolution of the same cycle at a deeper level. Your job is to keep praying them through it, every time, at every level.

Nehemiah built that wall with one hand while fighting the enemy with the other. That image is the picture of intercession. You're building something with your prayers, the spiritual structure of a person's life, the walls of protection around a family, the gates of purpose for a church.

And at the same time, you're fighting. Three spirits came against Nehemiah to pull him off the wall. The spirit of Sanballat brought discouragement. The spirit of Tobiah brought slander and mockery. The Ashtodite spirit brought confusion. All three of these will come against you as a watchman, especially when you're praying someone through a critical transition in the cycle. The enemy knows that if he can get you off the wall, the person you're praying for loses their intercessor and gets stuck. Stay on the wall. No matter how long it's been. No matter what you haven't seen yet. The wall is being built, gate by gate, prayer by prayer.

One more thing to understand before we walk through the specific gates. Your spiritual influence, your *metron*, determines who you have authority to pray for in this way. You can't just pick random people across the world and try to push them through the cycle with your prayers. Your authority in the spirit is tied to your relational assignment. The people in your household, your local church, your close relationships, the ones God has specifically placed in your sphere, these are the people your intercession carries the most weight for. Pray for others, absolutely. But know that your deepest, most authoritative intercession is reserved for the people God has specifically given you to guard. That's where you carry the most weight, and that's where your prayers do the most work.

From the Sheep Gate to the Old Gate

The first gate Nehemiah rebuilt was the Sheep Gate. In the natural, this was the gate through which the sheep were brought into Jerusalem for sacrifice at the temple. In the prophetic picture of the soul's journey, the Sheep Gate represents salvation. It's the entry point. It's the moment when a person recognizes Jesus as the Lamb of God, the sacrifice for their sin, and steps through the gate of new birth. Every other gate in the cycle depends on this one being open first. You can't disciple someone who hasn't been saved. You can't bring someone into maturity in Christ if they've never come to Christ. The Sheep Gate is where everything begins.

This is why every watchman must carry a deep desire to see souls saved. Not just a passive hope that people will eventually find their way to God, but a burning, active, prayerful burden for the lost. The *Shamar* anointing isn't just about guarding what's already inside the walls. It's about praying people through the gate in the first place. If you're called to intercession and you've lost your passion for the salvation of souls, ask God to restore it. Because the whole roadmap starts here, and without this gate, none of the others matter.

When you're praying for someone who isn't yet saved, your specific prayer focus at the Sheep Gate is this: pray that the grace of God draws them. Pray that the spirit of conviction falls on them. Pray that every spiritual blindness over their mind is broken in the name of Jesus. Pray that the right person, the right conversation, the right moment crosses their path. You're not just asking God to save them in a general way. You're standing at the Sheep Gate and decreeing it open for them, pushing them toward the threshold through your intercession until they step through.

The second gate is the Fish Gate. In Nehemiah's Jerusalem, the Fish Gate was where the fishermen brought their catch into the city. It was the gate of provision, of harvest, of bringing in what had been caught. In the prophetic roadmap, the Fish Gate represents discipleship. It's the stage where a new believer is caught up in the net of the Word, of community, of spiritual formation. It's where someone goes from simply being saved to being trained, taught, and shaped in their faith.

Discipleship is where many believers stall. They get saved and then nobody pours into them. Nobody walks with them through the Word. Nobody helps them understand what it means to pray, to fast, to resist temptation, to grow in the character of Christ. Without discipleship, a new believer is like a fish that got caught and then got thrown back in the water with no direction. They're saved, but they're not growing. They're at the Fish Gate, but nobody's walking them through it.

When you're interceding for someone at the Fish Gate, your prayer focus shifts. You're not praying for their salvation anymore. They're through that gate. Now you're praying specifically for their discipleship. Pray that God sends them a mentor, a spiritual father or mother, someone who will pour into them. Pray that they develop a hunger for the Word that doesn't go away. Pray that the spirit of religion doesn't get to them before the spirit of relationship does. Pray that they find a local church that will actually disciple them and not just entertain them. These are specific, targeted prayers for someone at a specific gate. That's the difference between generic intercession and watchman-level intercession.

The third gate is the Old Gate. The Old Gate in Jerusalem was one of the most ancient structures in the city. It represented what had stood the test of time, the things that had been proven true through generations. In the prophetic roadmap, the Old Gate represents maturity. It's the stage where a believer has been discipled, has gone through seasons of growth and testing, and has developed a settled, proven faith. They're not tossed around by every wind of doctrine. They're not shaken by every trial. They know who they are in God, and that knowledge has been forged through experience, not just information.

Maturity in the faith isn't automatic. It doesn't come just because someone has been saved for a long time. There are believers who have been in church for twenty years and are still spiritually immature because they've never allowed the process of God to do its full work in them. The Old Gate requires that a person has been through the gates before it, that they've been saved, discipled, and then pushed through the harder stages of the cycle that come next. Without proper intercession, people resist the process of maturity. They want the blessings of the Water Gate without going through the Valley Gate. They want the purpose without the purging. Your prayers are what help them stay in the process long enough for God to bring them to the Old Gate.

When you're praying for someone at the Old Gate, your focus is on their settling and their deepening. Pray that the Word of God becomes the foundation of everything they think and decide. Pray that the fear of the Lord grows in them, not fear as in terror, but the reverent, holy awareness that God is real and His ways are right. Pray that they don't get distracted by lesser things when God is trying to bring them into greater depth. Pray that every spirit of spiritual pride that tries to attach itself to their maturity gets cut off, because maturity without humility is just religious arrogance. True maturity looks like Christ, and Christ was the most humble person who ever walked the earth.

Now, here's where the roadmap gets harder, and where your intercession becomes most critical. After the Old Gate comes the Valley Gate. The Valley Gate represents the season of hardship that God allows in the life of a maturing believer. It's not punishment. It's purification. God looks into the heart of someone who is growing in Him and sees things that don't belong there. Idols. Pride. Self-reliance. Old mindsets. Things that were never supposed to be there, things that will actually prevent the person from walking in their full destiny if they stay. And so God, in His love and wisdom, allows a valley. A season of difficulty, loss, pressure, or pain that is specifically designed to bring those things to the surface so they can be removed.

David understood this. He said, "Search me, O God, and know my heart." The Valley Gate is God's answer to that prayer. He searches, He finds what shouldn't be there, and He uses the valley to bring it out. The valley isn't there to kill you. It's there to free you. The crushing isn't destruction. It's deliverance. But here's the problem: most people don't know that when they're in the valley. They think God has abandoned them. They think they're being punished. They think something has gone terribly wrong. And without a watchman praying them through, they can get stuck in the valley for years, going around the same mountain over and over, never getting to the gate on the other side.

After the Valley Gate comes the Dung Gate. This is the gate that nobody wants to talk about, but it's one of the most important in the entire roadmap. In Jerusalem, the Dung Gate was exactly what it sounds like. It was where the waste went out of the city. Everything that didn't belong inside the walls was carried out through this gate and disposed of. In the prophetic picture, the Dung Gate represents the moment of release. After going through the valley and having what shouldn't be in your heart brought to the surface, you come to the Dung Gate and you let it go. You drop off the old self. You release the bitterness. You surrender the idol. You let God take out everything the valley was designed to remove.

The prodigal son's moment in the pigpen is the Dung Gate experience. He was surrounded by waste. He was at his lowest. And that's exactly where he came to himself, where he finally let go of the life he had been holding onto and turned back toward the father. The pigpen wasn't the end of his story. It was the turning point. But without that moment of release, he never gets home.

People can get stuck at the Dung Gate for a very long time. They've been through the valley, they've had things brought to the surface, but they won't let go. They hold onto the offense. They hold onto the old identity. They hold onto the thing God is trying to remove because it's familiar, even if it's destructive. This is where your intercession is absolutely critical. Pray that the grace of God gives them the strength to release what needs to go. Pray that they don't turn the valley into a permanent address. Pray that God's goodness leads them to repentance, because Romans 2:4 says that's exactly what His goodness does. Decree that the chains of the old life are broken. Decree that what the enemy meant to keep them bound to is cut off in the name of Jesus.

After the Dung Gate comes the Fountain Gate. This is one of the most beautiful gates in the entire roadmap. After the valley, after the release, after the purging, God comes with a fresh filling. The Fountain Gate represents the moment when God refills what He emptied. He baptizes the person afresh in His Spirit. He gives them fresh vision. He restores what the valley took and adds to it what could only come after the purging. Jesus said in John 4, "Whoever drinks of the water I give them will never thirst again." The Fountain Gate is that living water. It's the refreshing that comes when the old has been removed and there's room for the new.

When you're praying for someone at the Fountain Gate, your specific prayer is for the fresh filling of the Holy Spirit. Pray that God pours out His Spirit on them in a new way. Pray that they receive fresh vision for their life and their calling. Pray that the joy of the Lord is restored to them, because after a valley, joy is often the first thing that needs to come back. Pray that they don't just receive the filling and then go back to old patterns. Pray that the fresh vision God gives them takes root and becomes the foundation for what comes next.

The Water Gate follows the Fountain Gate, and it represents the rebirthing of divine purpose. This is where a person steps into what God actually designed them for. Not just saved, not just discipled, not just mature, but walking in the specific assignment God wrote in the book about them before they were born. The Water Gate is where destiny becomes active. It's where the gifts God placed in them start to flow out to others. It's where they stop being primarily a receiver of ministry and start becoming a carrier of it.

Praying someone into the Water Gate is some of the most rewarding intercession you'll ever do. You're praying them into purpose. Pray that every assignment God wrote over their life before they were born comes to life in this season. Pray that they have the courage to step into what God is showing them, even when it's bigger than they feel ready for. Pray that the right doors open and the wrong ones close. Pray that they're surrounded by people who can recognize the gift on their life and call it out, not compete with it.

The gates that follow the Water Gate carry an eschatological weight. The Horse Gate represents the end times, the urgency of the hour we're living in. The East Gate represents the return of Jesus, who Scripture says will come through the eastern gate. The Inspection Gate represents the Great White Throne Judgment, where every person will stand before God and give an account. These final gates remind us that this whole roadmap isn't just about personal spiritual growth. It's about readiness. Without maturity, without going through the valley, without being filled afresh, without walking in divine purpose, a person won't be ready for what's coming. The watchman's intercession is ultimately about getting people ready for the return of the King. That's the weight behind every prayer you pray for every person in your sphere. You're not just helping them feel better about their life. You're pushing them toward eternal readiness.

Consider this hypothetical scenario to make the roadmap concrete. Imagine a woman named Kezia, a 36-year-old who has been saved for twelve years. She loves God, she serves in her church, she reads her Bible. But for the past three years she's felt like she's going around in circles. She went through a painful divorce. She lost a job she loved. She watched a close friendship end in betrayal.

She's been in a valley, but she doesn't know it's a valley. She thinks something is wrong with her faith. She's at the Valley Gate moving toward the Dung Gate, but she's been holding on to the bitterness from the divorce and the betrayal, unable to release it, unable to move forward. Now imagine a watchman in her life who has this roadmap. That watchman doesn't just pray a general prayer for Kezia. They see exactly where she is. And they begin to pray specifically that the spirit of unforgiveness is broken off her heart, that the grace of God gives her the strength to release what she's been carrying, and that she comes to the Dung Gate and drops it off so she can receive the fresh filling waiting for her on the other side. That kind of targeted prayer is what moves Kezia forward. That's the Nehemiah Intercession Roadmap in action.

Your Next Move

The roadmap is in your hands now. The question isn't whether you believe it works. The question is whether you'll use it. And using it starts with one very specific exercise that you need to do before you do anything else.

Get a piece of paper or open a notes app. Write down three people you're currently praying for. Not a list of twenty. Three. The people who are most consistently on your heart, the ones you wake up thinking about, the ones you feel the most burden for. Write their names down.

Now, for each person, go through the gates. The Sheep Gate is salvation. The Fish Gate is discipleship. The Old Gate is maturity. The Valley Gate is hardship and purification. The Dung Gate is the moment of release. The Fountain Gate is fresh filling and vision. The Water Gate is divine purpose. Look at what you know about each person's spiritual life right now and honestly identify which gate they're at. Don't overthink it. You know these people. You've been praying for them. Ask the Holy Spirit to confirm it and He will. And if you're not sure, make that your prayer: "God, show me where they are so I know how to pray."

Once you've identified the gate for each person, write down one specific prayer point for each one based on where they are. Not a general prayer. A specific one. If they're at the Sheep Gate, your prayer point is for the grace of God to draw them and for spiritual blindness to break. If they're at the Valley Gate, your prayer point is for endurance and understanding, that they would know the valley is not punishment but preparation. If they're at the Dung Gate, your prayer point is for the grace to release what God has been trying to remove. Write it down. Specific. Named. Targeted.

Then pray those three prayers every day this week. Not a long, elaborate prayer session. Three specific, faith-filled decrees over three specific people at three specific gates. Five minutes of targeted intercession done consistently will accomplish more than an hour of vague, unfocused prayer. James 5:16 says the effective prayer of a righteous person accomplishes much. The key word is effective. Effective prayer is aimed prayer. It knows what it's pushing toward and it pushes.

When you pray, don't beg. Don't approach God as if He needs to be convinced to care about the people you're praying for. He cares more than you do. You're not informing God of a problem He doesn't know about. You're standing as a son or daughter before a Father who has already declared His will, and you're legislating that will into the natural realm. Come with boldness. Come with the confidence of someone who knows they're standing in the gap for a specific assignment. You're not a beggar. You're an ambassador. You're part of the government of God. You legislate. You decree. You push people forward in the roadmap with the authority of heaven behind you.

The *Shamar* anointing over your family and your city is built one gate at a time, one prayer at a time, one person at a time. Nobody moves through the cycle alone. Somebody has to be standing in the gap. That's why you're here. That's why this call is on your life. The wall doesn't build itself, and the gates don't open on their own. But with a watchman standing in prayer, pushing people forward with precision and authority, things move. People come home. Valleys end. Purpose is birthed. Gates open. And the King finds His people ready when He returns.

Activation & Reflection

---

1. What broken walls in your family, church, or community is God calling you to rebuild through intercession?

____

____

____

____

2. How does Nehemiah's pattern — mourning, fasting, confessing, and asking boldly — challenge your current approach to prayer?

____

____

____

____

3. What is one specific area where God has given you a roadmap in prayer that you have yet to fully act upon?

____

____

____

____

4. Like Nehemiah, who are the people God has placed around you to partner with in rebuilding through prayer?

____

____

____

____

5. What opposition are you currently facing in your intercessory work, and how will you respond to it the way Nehemiah responded?

____

____

____

____

A Prayer of Rebuilding

God of Nehemiah, I come before You with a broken heart for what has been broken in my world. I weep over the walls that have fallen. I confess the sins of neglect and prayerlessness. Grant me Your blueprint for rebuilding. Raise up laborers who will stand beside me at the wall. And when opposition rises, let me not stop to negotiate with the enemy — let me keep building. In Jesus' name, Amen.

CHAPTER 3

The Valley and the Dung Gate

The Purpose of the Crushing

There's a gate in Nehemiah's roadmap that nobody volunteers for. Nobody wakes up and says, "I can't wait to go through the Valley Gate today." But every mature believer who has ever walked with God for any serious length of time knows exactly what it feels like to be in that valley. The pressure that won't lift. The season that seems to have no end. The silence from heaven that makes you wonder if God is even paying attention. That's the Valley Gate. And if you don't understand what it's actually for, it will break you instead of build you.

The Valley Gate in Nehemiah 3 wasn't a side entrance. It was a real, functioning gate in the wall of Jerusalem. People passed through it. It had a purpose. And in the prophetic roadmap of the soul's journey, the Valley Gate represents the season of hardship that God allows in the life of a maturing believer. Not as punishment. Not because He's forgotten you. But because He looked inside your heart and found something that doesn't belong there, something that will actually block you from carrying what He wants to give you next.

That's the key phrase. What comes next.

God doesn't send you into a valley to destroy you. He sends you into a valley to prepare you for what you couldn't carry before. A mature believer who hasn't been through the valley is like a container that still has old contents in it. You can't pour something new and fresh into a vessel that's already full of something that shouldn't be there. The valley is God's way of emptying the vessel. And yes, the process feels like crushing. But crushing isn't the same as killing. The crushing is designed to deliver you from yourself, from the version of you that can't handle what God wants to release next.

David understood this deeply. In Psalm 139:23-24, he prayed, "Search me, O God, and know my heart. Test me and know my anxious thoughts. See if there is any offensive way in me, and lead me in the way everlasting." The Valley Gate is God's direct answer to that prayer. He searches. He finds what doesn't belong. And He uses the valley to bring it to the surface so it can be removed. The valley isn't a detour from your destiny. It's a required transit point on the way to it.

What kinds of things does God bring out through the valley? Pride that's been dressed up as confidence. Self-reliance that's been mistaken for faith. Idols that have been hiding behind ministry activity. Unforgiveness that's been stored in places you didn't even know it was living. Offenses that you thought you'd dealt with but hadn't. Fear that's been masked by busyness. The valley strips the masks off. It brings everything to the surface. And that process is uncomfortable, sometimes deeply painful. But it's not random. Every bit of the pressure is targeted at something specific that God wants out of you.

This is also where spiritual warfare intensifies. When you're in the valley, three spirits will come at you the same way they came at Nehemiah on the wall. The first is the spirit of discouragement. It shows up and says, "Look how long you've been in this season. Nothing is changing. Why are you still praying? Why are you still believing? You've been faithful and look where it got you." That voice is a lie. The valley has a gate on both sides. There's a way in and there's a way out. The spirit of discouragement wants you to believe there's only a way in. Don't believe it.

The second spirit is the one that slanders your identity while you're in the valley. It tells you that the reason you're going through hard things is because something is fundamentally wrong with you, that you're not called, not anointed, not good enough, not worthy of what you were believing for. This spirit uses the vulnerability of the valley to attack who you are. It knows that if it can get you to doubt your identity while you're in the hard season, you'll come out of the valley without the confidence to walk into what God prepared for you on the other side.

The third is the spirit of confusion. It clouds your thinking so that you can't see clearly what God is doing. You start questioning everything. Was that really God's voice? Did I miss a turn somewhere? Is this valley my fault? That confusion is designed to make you misinterpret the valley as punishment rather than preparation. When you're confused about why you're in the valley, you can't cooperate with what God is trying to do in it. You fight the process instead of submitting to it. And fighting the process makes the valley longer.

The fastest way through the valley is actually counterintuitive. David said it plainly: if you can get to a place where you examine your own heart and understand why you're there, the season can speed up. Knowledge of the purpose accelerates the process. When you stop asking "Why is this happening to me?" and start asking "God, what are you delivering me from?" the whole dynamic shifts. You go from resisting the valley to cooperating with it. And a believer who cooperates with God's purification process moves through the valley far faster than one who fights it every step of the way.

So here's the specific practice for navigating the Valley Gate with wisdom. When you're in a hard season, set aside time to sit before God with one direct question: "What are you delivering me from?" Not "when will this end?" and not "why is this happening?" Those questions focus on the circumstances. The right question focuses on the purpose. Get a journal. Write the question at the top of the page. Then sit in silence and let God answer. He will. He might bring a specific memory to mind. He might surface a pattern you've been repeating. He might show you a relationship you've been holding onto that's been pulling you away from Him. Whatever He shows you, write it down. That's not just journaling. That's spiritual intelligence. That's you locating the target of the valley so you can cooperate with God instead of fighting Him.

Once you identify what God is delivering you from, pray into it specifically. Don't pray around it. Pray directly at it. If it's pride, say out loud, "God, I surrender my need to be right. I surrender my need to be seen. I release pride from my heart right now in the name of Jesus." If it's a specific fear, name it and release it. If it's an idol, call it what it is and hand it over. The valley doesn't end when the circumstances change. The valley ends when what it was designed to remove has actually been removed. That's when God opens the next gate.

And as a watchman, you're not just navigating your own valleys. You're praying other people through theirs. When you see someone in your sphere going through a hard season, your intercession isn't just "God, help them." Your intercession is targeted. You're asking God to show you what He's trying to deliver them from, and then you're standing in the gap, decreeing that the purpose of the valley is fulfilled, that the crushing does its work, and that they come out the other side carrying less of what shouldn't be there and more of what God intended for them all along.

Dropping the Old Self

After the Valley Gate comes a gate that most people don't want to talk about. The Dung Gate. In Nehemiah's Jerusalem, this was the gate through which all the waste of the city was carried out. Everything that didn't belong inside the walls, everything that was used up, broken down, or corrupted, went out through this gate. It was not a glamorous gate. Nobody celebrated it. But without it, the city would have been buried in its own refuse. The Dung Gate was absolutely necessary.

In the prophetic roadmap, the Dung Gate represents the moment of release. After the valley has brought things to the surface, after the crushing has done its work, you arrive at this gate with a choice. You can drop off everything God pulled out of you during the valley. Or you can hold onto it.

Most people hold onto it.

This is one of the most common places believers get stuck. They go through the valley. They feel the pain. They survive the hard season. But when they get to the Dung Gate, they can't let go. They carry the bitterness from the relationship that broke. They hold onto the old identity that the valley was supposed to remove. They keep the wound close because at least it's familiar. They replay the offense over and over. They rehearse the disappointment. They wear the old garment of who they used to be because even though it's filthy, it fits. It's known. And the unknown on the other side of the Dung Gate feels too uncertain to step into.

The prodigal son is the clearest picture of this in all of Scripture. He went through a valley, a real one, a season of complete loss and humiliation. He ended up in a pigpen, surrounded by waste, eating what the pigs ate. That's the Dung Gate experience in the most vivid possible terms. But the Bible says that while he was there, he "came to himself." Something broke. The old version of him, the one that had demanded his inheritance and walked away from his father, finally cracked open. And in that moment, he made a decision. He got up. He turned around. He went home.

But consider how many people are still sitting in the pigpen right now. They've been through the valley. They know something needs to change. But they can't get up. They can't let go. They're having what could be called a pity party at the Dung Gate, sitting in the middle of everything God was trying to remove, too comfortable in their misery to move toward the freedom waiting on the other side. Without a watchman standing in the gap for them, people can stay in that pigpen for years. Decades. Some stay there for the rest of their lives.

That's the weight of the intercessor's call at this gate. Your prayers are what break the pity party. Your decrees are what lift the spirit of heaviness that keeps people glued to the Dung Gate. When you pray for someone stuck here, you're not praying a soft, gentle prayer. You're praying a targeted, authoritative decree that the chains holding them to the old life are broken right now in the name of Jesus. You're decreeing that the grace of God gives them the strength to stand up, turn around, and walk through the gate. You're standing in the gap between where they are and where God is calling them, and you're pulling them forward through intercession.

Think about a man named Jerome, a 44-year-old who gave his life to Christ after years of addiction and broken relationships. He got saved. He got discipled. He grew in his faith. Then a painful church split happened, one that involved accusations against his character that weren't true. He went through the valley hard. The betrayal was real. The damage was real. But now, two years later, Jerome is still talking about what happened. He's still carrying the wound. He's still defined by the offense. Every time God tries to open a new door for him, Jerome walks back to the pigpen and sits down again. He's at the Dung Gate, and he won't let go. What Jerome needs isn't more sympathy. He needs an intercessor who will stand in the gap and decree that the spirit of offense is broken off his soul, that the grace of God empowers him to release what he's been holding, and that the identity God wrote over him before he was born is more real than the identity the betrayal tried to give him.

For your own life, when you find yourself at the Dung Gate, here's the specific practice that moves you through it. First, name what you're carrying. Don't be vague with God. He already knows what it is. But there's power in you naming it out loud. "I am carrying bitterness toward this person. I am carrying shame from this season. I am carrying the old identity that says I'm not enough." Name it specifically. Then make a verbal declaration, out loud, not just in your head. Say these words or words like them: "I am dropping this at the Dung Gate today. This does not belong in my future. I release it right now in the name of Jesus, and I refuse to pick it back up." Say it like you mean it. Because you do. And then walk through the gate without looking back.

That verbal declaration matters more than most believers realize. Romans 10:10 says that with the mouth, confession is made. There's a reason God designed confession as a spoken act. When you speak a release out loud, you're not just expressing an emotion. You're making a spiritual decree. You're issuing a legal statement in the spirit that the old thing no longer has a claim on you. The enemy has no legal right to keep you at the Dung Gate once you've made that declaration through the blood of Jesus. He has to let go. The gate opens. And you walk through.

As a watchman interceding for others at this gate, your prayer focus is specific. Pray that God's goodness leads them to repentance, because Romans 2:4 says that's exactly how it works. His goodness, not His judgment, is what draws people to release. Pray that every spirit of heaviness that's been keeping them in the pity party is broken off right now. Pray that the Father's love becomes more real to them than the pain they've been living in. Pray that they receive the grace to stand up and walk through the gate. And decree, don't just ask, decree that the chains are broken and that the old garment falls off in the name of Jesus.

One more thing about the Dung Gate that's crucial for watchmen to understand. Sometimes the thing a person needs to drop at this gate isn't just an offense or a wound. Sometimes it's an old calling, an old assignment, an old version of their ministry that God is done with. He's trying to take them into something new, but they're holding onto the old thing because it was good, because it bore fruit, because it was real. But it was for a season. And now the season is over. The Dung Gate asks you to release even the good things that God has completed, not just the bad things He's removed. That can be the hardest release of all. But it's the one that opens the door to the Fountain Gate, and what waits on the other side of that gate is worth every moment of letting go.

The Refreshing of the Fountain Gate

After the valley. After the release. After the hardest gates in the entire roadmap. God does something that is so like Him it almost takes your breath away. He fills you back up.

The Fountain Gate in Nehemiah's Jerusalem was the gate closest to the water source, the spring that fed the city. It was the gate of refreshing, of life, of supply. In the prophetic roadmap, the Fountain Gate represents the glory moment of God refilling what the valley emptied. It's the fresh baptism of the Holy Spirit that comes after the purging. It's the new vision, the new purpose, the new joy that God pours into a vessel that has been emptied of what didn't belong and is now ready to be filled with what does.

God never leaves a void. That's one of the most important things you need to understand about how He works. When He removes something from your heart through the valley, He doesn't just leave an empty space and walk away. He fills it. Jesus said in John 4:14, "Whoever drinks of the water that I shall give him will never thirst again. The water that I shall give him will become in him a fountain of water springing up into everlasting life." The Fountain Gate is that promise made real in the experience of a believer who has just come through the valley and the dung gate. They're empty of the old. And now God comes with living water and fills them to overflowing.

This is also where the Word of God becomes a cleansing agent in a way that goes deeper than before. Think about what happened in the outer courts of Moses' tabernacle. There was a laven of water where the priests would wash before entering the presence of God. They would look into the water and wash their hands, their face, their feet. But the only reflection in that water was their own. They could wash the outside, but the inside, the soul, the mind, the deep places of the heart, those couldn't be reached by that water. That's why Jesus said, "I am the living water." When you drink of Him, when you saturate yourself in the Word of God after coming through the valley, something happens that no external washing can produce. Your mind gets washed. Your desires change. The things you used to want, the things the valley was designed to remove, you don't want them anymore. The Word does what the laven couldn't. It sanctifies from the inside out.

The Samaritan woman in John 4 is one of the clearest pictures of the Fountain Gate in action. She came to the well broken, defined by her history, carrying an identity that had been shaped by every failed relationship and every compromise she'd ever made. She was at the Dung Gate in her soul, still carrying everything that shouldn't be there. And then she met Jesus. And He gave her living water. Not just a spiritual experience. A transformation of mind and desire. She left that well and she didn't want what she used to want. She became an evangelist. She went back into her city and won people to God. The woman who used to go to the well at noon to avoid people because of her shame was now the person calling the whole city to come and see the Messiah. The Fountain Gate changed everything about her. Not because she worked harder. But because she got filled with something new.

For you personally, seeking the refreshing of the Fountain Gate after every season of trial is not optional. It's essential. A watchman who goes through the valley, drops off the old at the Dung Gate, and then just keeps moving without stopping at the Fountain Gate will walk in a dry spirit. They'll be emptied but not filled. And an empty vessel doesn't carry anything to anyone. The Fountain Gate is where you receive what you need to be effective again. It's where God restores your joy, your vision, your hunger for

Him, your sense of purpose. You can't skip it. You can't rush past it. You have to stop and drink.

Here's the specific practice for seeking the Fountain Gate after a hard season. Block out an extended time with God, not your regular prayer time, but a longer, intentional time of just being with Him. Two hours. Three hours. A full day if you can. Come with your Bible and a journal. Begin by thanking God out loud for what He delivered you from in the valley. Name it specifically. "God, thank you for removing the pride that was blocking my next season. Thank you for delivering me from the bitterness I was carrying." Gratitude opens the gate. Then ask Him directly: "God, what do you want to fill me with now?" And wait. Read through a passage of Scripture slowly and let it speak. Write down what the Holy Spirit highlights. Ask God for fresh vision, not a general sense of things being okay, but a specific picture of what He's calling you into next. Write that down too. Then pray in the Spirit, allowing the Holy Spirit to pray through you what your own words can't fully express. Stay until you feel the shift. You'll know when the Fountain Gate has opened. There's a specific sense of refreshing, of clarity, of renewed desire for God that comes when you've truly received the filling He has for you.

As a watchman interceding for others at the Fountain Gate, your prayer shifts again. You're not praying for their endurance anymore. You're not praying for their release. You're praying for their filling. Pray that the Holy Spirit comes upon them with fresh fire. Pray that God gives them a specific vision for the next season of their life, something concrete enough to hold onto and move toward. Pray that their hunger for God is restored, because after a valley, hunger is often the first casualty. Pray that they don't just receive the filling and then go back to old patterns, but that the fresh vision God gives them becomes the foundation for the Water Gate, for the divine purpose that's waiting on the other side.

There's something else that happens at the Fountain Gate that watchmen need to understand. This is where God begins to remind you of the promises He put in your heart before the valley started. The desires He placed in you when you were young. The words He spoke over you in seasons of intimacy. The vision He gave you before the hard season tried to bury it. At the Fountain Gate, God says, "Remember what I told you? I haven't forgotten it. I haven't changed my mind. The valley didn't cancel the promise. It prepared you to carry it." And when those promises come back to life at the Fountain Gate, they come back with more weight, more clarity, and more authority than they had before, because now you've been emptied of what would have corrupted them and filled with what will carry them.

Psalm 41:1-3 says, "Blessed is he who considers the poor. The Lord will deliver him in time of trouble. The Lord will preserve him and keep him alive, and he will be blessed on the earth. The Lord will strengthen him on his bed of illness." This is the promise of the Fountain Gate for those who have gone through the valley with their hands open.

God doesn't just restore. He preserves. He keeps alive. He strengthens. The Fountain Gate isn't just about feeling better after a hard season. It's about being repositioned with fresh strength and fresh purpose for what God is about to do next.

Watchmen who understand the Fountain Gate also understand something about the atmosphere they carry. After going through the valley, dropping the old at the Dung Gate, and being filled afresh at the Fountain Gate, something changes about the spiritual atmosphere around you. You don't just pray for breakthrough anymore. You carry it. The woman at the well didn't just get her own life changed. She created an atmosphere in her city that drew people to Jesus. That's what the Fountain Gate produces in a watchman. A freshly filled vessel doesn't just benefit itself. It overflows. It creates a cloud. Everywhere you go, people encounter what you're carrying, and what you're carrying is the fresh presence of God that came after the valley did its work.

That's the *Shamar* anointing at its most powerful. Not the anointing of someone who has never been through hard things. But the anointing of someone who went through the valley, dropped the old self at the Dung Gate, and came out the other side full of fresh fire and fresh purpose. That person doesn't just guard the gate. They change the atmosphere of every room they walk into. They don't pray for revival. They carry it. They don't ask God for breakthrough. They become the atmosphere of breakthrough for everyone in their sphere.

The Fountain Gate is available to you right now, no matter how long your valley has been or how much you're still carrying at the Dung Gate. God's invitation to drink from living water doesn't expire. It doesn't run out. It doesn't require you to have it all together before you come. You come empty. You come broken. You come having just dropped off everything that shouldn't be there. And He fills you. That's who He is. That's what the Fountain Gate is for.

Putting It Into Practice

Three gates. Three distinct stages of God's work in a believer's life. And each one requires a different response from you, both in your own walk and in your intercession for others.

Start by doing an honest assessment of where you currently are. Not where you want to be. Where you actually are. Ask yourself three questions and write down your answers. First: am I in a valley right now, and if so, have I asked God what He is delivering me from? Second: is there something I'm still carrying that belongs at the Dung Gate, an offense, an old identity, an old assignment, a wound I haven't released? Third: when did I last seek the Fountain Gate, a genuine, extended time of asking God to fill me fresh with His Spirit and His vision? Your answers to these three questions will tell you exactly where you are in the cycle and what your next step needs to be.

If you're in the valley, do this today. Set aside thirty minutes, sit before God, and write this question at the top of a page: "God, what are you delivering me from in this season?" Then sit in silence and write down everything that comes. Don't filter it. Don't edit it. Just write. When you have your answer, pray into it directly and specifically by name. Don't pray around it. Pray at it. Decree that the valley does its full work and that you come out of it carrying less of what shouldn't be there and more of what God intended.

If you're at the Dung Gate, make a verbal declaration today. Out loud. Specific. Name what you're releasing and declare that it has no more claim on your future. Do it once. Do it with conviction. And then refuse to pick it back up. Every time the enemy tries to hand it back to you, you say the same thing: "I dropped that at the Dung Gate. It doesn't belong to me anymore."

If you haven't sought the Fountain Gate in a while, schedule it this week. A real, extended time with God. Not a quick prayer before work. A block of time where you come before Him with your Bible, your journal, and one question: "God, what do you want to fill me with now?" Come expecting an answer. Come expecting a fresh filling. Come expecting that God will remind you of promises He hasn't forgotten, even if you have.

For your intercession, take the three people you identified in the previous chapter and locate them at these gates. Is any of them in a valley right now? Pray specifically that they cooperate with God's process and come through it carrying less of what shouldn't be there. Is anyone stuck at the Dung Gate? Decree that the chains are broken and that the grace of God empowers them to release what they've been holding. Is anyone ready for the Fountain Gate? Pray a fresh filling of the Holy Spirit over them and ask God to give them fresh vision for their next season.

Write these prayers down. One sentence per person. Specific. Named. Targeted. Then pray them every day this week. Not long elaborate prayers. Short, precise, faith-filled decrees over people you know are in a specific place in the cycle. That's watchman-level intercession. That's the *Shamar* anointing at work over the people God has placed in your care.

The valley doesn't last forever. The Dung Gate is not a permanent address. And the Fountain Gate is always open for those who come empty and ready to receive. God is faithful to complete the work He started. Your job is to cooperate with it in your own life and to stand in the gap for the people in your sphere until they do the same.

Activation & Reflection

---

1. What valleys — seasons of humiliation, failure, or confusion — has God allowed in your life that have actually purified your intercession?

____

____

____

____

2. The Dung Gate represents the place where waste is removed. What spiritual waste — bitterness, pride, unresolved sin — needs to be cleared from your life to make you a cleaner vessel of prayer?

____

____

____

____

3. How have you seen God bring refreshing (the Fountain Gate) after a season of crushing?

____

____

____

____

4. What does it mean to you personally that God often begins His restoration work in the valleys, not on the mountaintops?

____
____
____
____

5. Write a brief release — surrendering the wound, shame, or offense you have been carrying into God's hands. What are you letting go of today?

____
____
____
____

A Prayer of Release

Father, I bring every valley experience before You — every wound, every failure, every humiliation I have carried too long. I pass them through the Dung Gate today, releasing the residue of shame, bitterness, and disappointment. Cleanse me thoroughly. Bring me to the Fountain Gate of refreshing. Let the crushing produce wine, not wasted time. Restore the joy of my salvation. In Jesus' name, Amen.

CHAPTER 4

Purpose, Rapture, and Judgment

Every gate Nehemiah rebuilt was leading somewhere. The Sheep Gate, the Fish Gate, the Old Gate, the Valley Gate, the Dung Gate, the Fountain Gate, the Water Gate. Each one was a step in the cycle. Each one prepared a person for what came next. But the roadmap doesn't end at the Water Gate. There are gates beyond it that carry a weight unlike anything that came before. These aren't gates about personal growth or spiritual formation. These are gates about eternity. They're about the return of a King, the end of an age, and the moment every one of us will stand before a sovereign God and give an account for what we did with what He gave us.

That's where this chapter lives.

If you've walked through the earlier gates, if you've survived the valley, dropped the old self at the Dung Gate, and received the fresh filling of the Fountain Gate, then you've arrived at a place where God can actually use you at a kingdom level. The Water Gate is where purpose gets reborn. But the gates that follow it are where that purpose finds its ultimate context. They connect your daily prayer life to something much larger than your personal story. They connect the *Shamar* anointing you carry to the most significant event in all of human history: the return of Jesus Christ.

A watchman who doesn't have one eye on the return of the King is only doing half the job.

The Rebirthing of Destiny

The Water Gate is where everything you went through finally makes sense.

Think about what the journey looked like to get here. You got saved at the Sheep Gate. You were discipled at the Fish Gate. You grew into maturity at the Old Gate. Then God allowed the valley, not to punish you, but to strip away what didn't belong. You dropped the old self at the Dung Gate. You received the fresh filling at the Fountain Gate. And now you're standing at the Water Gate, the gate of rebirthing, the gate where God says, "Now. Now you're ready. Now I can give you back your purpose with nothing in the way to corrupt it."

The Water Gate represents the rebirthing of divine purpose. It's not just a return to what you were doing before the valley. It's the original assignment God wrote over your life before you were born, coming alive in a new way, with new clarity, new authority, and new capacity to carry it. The valley didn't cancel your destiny. It prepared you to handle it without dropping it.

Psalm 139 tells us that God wrote a book about each of us before we took our first breath. Every day of our lives was recorded before one of them came to be. That means before you ever went through your first hard season, before your first failure, before your first valley, God had already written the full story. He knew what the valley would take out of you. He knew what the Dung Gate would remove. He knew what the Fountain Gate would pour in. And He knew what the Water Gate would birth. The whole process was in the book before you even started.

This is why purpose is one of the most powerful forces in a human life. When you know what God wrote about you, when those promises and desires that have been in your heart since childhood come back to life at the Water Gate, something shifts in how you carry yourself. You don't just pray anymore. You legislate. You stand before God and you say, "Remember what you told me. Remember what you placed in my heart. I haven't fulfilled it yet. I can't stop now." That's not arrogance. That's a son or daughter building a case from the promises of a Father who doesn't break His word.

There's a story in Scripture that captures this perfectly. The woman who couldn't have a child was given a prophetic promise by the man of God. A son was coming. And the son came. But when the boy grew older, he died suddenly. The woman didn't collapse in despair. She didn't accept it as final. She went straight to the man of God, and when she found him, she said something that carries the full weight of what it means to stand at the Water Gate. She said, "Did I ask you for a son? Did I say, give me a son?" She was reminding him of the prophecy. She was building a case from the promise. She was saying, "You spoke this over my life. It hasn't been fulfilled yet. So this can't be the end." And because of that declaration, because of that refusal to accept a conclusion that contradicted the promise, the boy was raised back to life. The power of resurrection came from the reminder of destiny.

That's what the Water Gate does for a watchman. It gives you back the promises that the valley tried to bury. It restores the original vision with a clarity you couldn't have had before you went through the process. And it positions you to carry your assignment with a level of authority that only comes after purification.

But here's what you need to understand about the Water Gate. You can't get there without the gates before it. You can't walk in true destiny until you've successfully navigated the valley and been refilled at the fountain. There's no shortcut. God doesn't allow a mature believer to bypass the valley because you can't take what's next while you're still holding onto what was. The crushing delivers you from the version of yourself that would misuse the purpose. The Dung Gate removes the things that would corrupt the assignment. The Fountain Gate fills you with what you need to carry it. And then, only then, does the Water Gate open.

This is also where three specific spirits will make their final push to keep you from stepping through. The spirit of discouragement will tell you that you've been waiting too long, that your time has passed, that other people have already stepped into what you were supposed to do. The spirit of slander will attack your character and try to make others doubt who you are right before God is about to use you in a significant way. And the spirit of confusion will cloud your thinking about your assignment, making you second-guess what God clearly told you, making you feel unqualified right at the moment you're most ready. All three of these spirits show up at the Water Gate because the enemy knows what's on the other side of it. He knows that a believer who has been through the valley, emptied at the Dung Gate, filled at the Fountain Gate, and now stepping into divine purpose is one of the most dangerous forces in the kingdom of God.

Don't let him stop you at the last gate before destiny.

David was called at seventeen. He didn't reign until he was thirty-three. Sixteen years between the anointing and the throne. Sixteen years of valleys, of running, of waiting, of being misunderstood, of watching lesser men sit in the seat that was already his. But David stayed in the process. He didn't try to force the door open ahead of God's timing. He didn't allow the enemy to devalue his importance during the waiting. And when God punched his card, when the time of recognition came, David was exactly where he needed to be to receive it. Promotion only comes from the Lord. No man can punch that card. And the enemy's entire strategy during the waiting season is to get you so discouraged, so confused, so beaten down by slander, that you're not standing in your place when God opens the door.

Your time of recognition is coming. But you have to be present for it. You have to be on the wall when it arrives.

As a watchman, part of your assignment at the Water Gate is to pray other people into their purpose. There's not a single person walking in their God-given destiny who got there without someone standing in the gap for them. Not one. Every person in your sphere of influence is somewhere in this cycle. And many of them are stuck between the Valley Gate and the Dung Gate, going around the same mountain, unable to release what the valley was supposed to remove, never getting to the refreshing, never arriving at the Water Gate where their purpose is waiting. Your intercession is what pushes them through. Your prayers are the force that moves them from one gate to the next. You're not just praying for them to feel better. You're praying them into the fullness of what God wrote about them before they were born.

Think about a woman named Sonia, a 39-year-old who has been in ministry for over a decade. She's gifted. She's called. Everyone around her can see it. But Sonia has been in a holding pattern for three years. She went through a painful season where everything she built seemed to fall apart. She dropped most of the old things at the Dung Gate, but she's still holding onto one thing: the fear that if she steps fully into her purpose, she'll fail again the way she did before. She's right at the edge of the Water Gate, but she won't walk through it. She's not stuck in the valley anymore. She's not in the pigpen. She's standing at the door of her destiny and she's afraid to open it. What Sonia needs isn't more encouragement. She needs a watchman who will stand in the gap and decree that every spirit of fear attached to her past failure is broken off right now in the name of Jesus, that the courage God placed in her before the foundation of the world rises up in her today, and that the Water Gate opens wide for her in this season. That's targeted intercession. That's the *Shamar* anointing at work for someone standing on the edge of their destiny.

Here's what you need to do specifically when you're interceding for someone at the Water Gate. First, pray that God brings the original promises back to their memory. Ask the Holy Spirit to remind them of the desires He placed in their heart before the valley, the vision He gave them before the hard season tried to bury it. Second, decree that every spirit of fear, discouragement, and confusion that's been assigned to keep them from stepping through the gate is broken off right now in the name of Jesus. Third, pray that the right doors open at the right time and that they have the courage to walk through them when they do. Fourth, declare over them what God already declared in His book about them: that they are called, equipped, and ready, not because they feel ready, but because God says they are.

Write those four prayer points down. Speak them out loud over the specific people in your sphere who are at this gate. That's not a suggestion. That's the work of a watchman who understands what's at stake when someone is standing at the door of their divine purpose and needs someone to stand in the gap for them.

The East Gate and the Coming King

After the Water Gate comes the Horse Gate. In Nehemiah's Jerusalem, the Horse Gate was the gate through which the king's horses and chariots passed. It was the gate of military readiness, of royal movement, of the king preparing for action. In the prophetic roadmap, the Horse Gate represents the end times. The urgency of the hour we're living in. The awareness that history is moving toward a specific, predetermined conclusion, and that conclusion is closer than most believers want to think about.

And then comes the East Gate.

The East Gate is one of the most significant gates in all of Jerusalem's history. It's the gate that faces east, toward the Mount of Olives. It's the gate that, according to Ezekiel 44:2, was shut after the glory of the Lord passed through it, and God declared that it would remain shut because the Lord God of Israel had entered through it. Jewish tradition holds this gate sacred precisely because of that declaration. It's the gate through which the Messiah will enter when He returns. And Jesus, standing on the Mount of Olives in Matthew 24, looking toward that gate, told His disciples that the Son of Man would come in power and great glory.

Jesus is coming back through the East Gate.

That's not poetry. That's a prophetic reality that every watchman must hold in their spirit every single day. The East Gate in the Nehemiah roadmap represents the Rapture and the return of Jesus Christ. And the gap between where we are in the cycle right now and the moment He returns is very small. Smaller than most people realize. Smaller than the gap looks when you're comfortable in your daily routine. The urgency of the East Gate is that we are closer to the return of Christ than we have ever been, and the enemy knows it. That's why the attacks are intensifying. That's why the confusion is louder. That's why the pressure on families, on churches, and on intercessors is heavier than it's ever been. The enemy is working overtime because he knows his time is short.

God said in Ezekiel 22:30 that He looked for a man who would stand in the gap and found none. That verse should shake every one of us. We are approaching the coming of Christ and we've lost our desire to pray. That's the danger. Not just that the world is getting darker. The danger is that the people who are supposed to be standing in the gap are distracted, discouraged, and disconnected from the urgency of the hour. A watchman without urgency is just a person standing on a wall. The urgency of the East Gate is what turns a prayer life into a kingdom assignment.

Standing in the gap means more than just praying. It means positioning yourself between heaven and earth so that the things that are supposed to happen will happen and the things that are not supposed to happen will not happen. That's the full weight of what God was looking for in Ezekiel 22. Someone who would stand in both realms at once. Someone who would take hold of heaven's agenda and enforce it in the earth. Someone who would refuse to let the enemy's plans advance unchallenged. That's the watchman's call in the context of the East Gate. You're not just praying for your family and your church. You're praying in the context of eternity. You're interceding with the awareness that the return of the King is the ultimate destination of everything you're doing.

This changes the way you pray. When you know that Jesus is coming back, when you hold the East Gate in your spirit as the final destination of the roadmap, your intercession takes on a different weight. You're not just praying people through the cycle for their benefit. You're praying them through the cycle because without maturity and without divine purpose, they won't be ready for the Rapture. That's what's at stake. Not just a better life here. Eternal readiness. And that's the ultimate motivation behind every prayer a watchman prays.

Think about what it means that the gap between the teaching and the coming of Christ is narrow. Nehemiah's roadmap, the whole cycle from the Sheep Gate to the East Gate, represents the full journey of a soul from salvation to readiness for the return of the King. And in the actual layout of Jerusalem's walls, the East Gate sits very close to the end of the cycle. The gap is small. That's intentional. God is saying that the time between where we are and where this is all going is shorter than we think. The watchman who understands this doesn't pray with a casual, "whenever you're ready, God" attitude. The watchman who understands this prays with urgency, with focus, with the awareness that every person still stuck at the Valley Gate or sitting in the pigpen at the Dung Gate is running out of time to get to where they need to be.

The most dangerous thing that can happen to an intercessor in this hour is to lose the urgency of the East Gate. To get so comfortable in the routine of prayer, so focused on the personal and the immediate, that you forget what the whole thing is building toward. The return of Jesus is not a theological concept for Sunday mornings. It's the event that gives every prayer you pray its ultimate meaning. It's the reason the *Shamar* anointing matters. It's the reason standing in the gap matters. It's the reason you can't afford to come off the wall.

So here's what you need to do to keep the East Gate alive in your daily walk. Every time you sit down to pray, before you bring your list of needs and intercessions, take sixty seconds to acknowledge the East Gate out loud. Say something like this: "Lord, I pray today with the awareness that you are coming back. I pray with the urgency of a watchman who knows the time is short. Every prayer I pray, I pray in the context of eternity. Let my intercession today push people closer to readiness for your return." That's not a ritual. That's a repositioning. It shifts your prayer from being primarily about the present to being anchored in the eternal. And when your prayers are anchored in the eternal, they carry a different kind of weight.

You also need to pray specifically for the people in your sphere who aren't ready. Not just saved, but ready. There's a difference. Readiness for the return of Christ requires maturity and divine purpose. A person who's been saved for twenty years but has never come through the valley, never dropped the old self at the Dung Gate, never received the fresh filling of the Fountain Gate, and never stepped into their divine purpose at the Water Gate is saved but not ready in the fullest sense. Your intercession for them isn't just about their current struggles. It's about their eternal positioning. Pray them through the cycle with urgency, because the East Gate is closer than it looks.

The Inspection Gate: Giving an Account

The final gate in Nehemiah's roadmap is the Inspection Gate. And it's the one that should make every believer stop and get serious.

The Inspection Gate represents the Great White Throne Judgment. The moment described in Revelation 20 where every person stands before a sovereign God and gives an account. Not just unbelievers. Every person. Every believer will stand before the judgment seat of Christ and give an account of what they did with what He gave them. The gifts

He placed in them. The assignment He wrote in the book. The people He put in their sphere. The prayers He called them to pray. The gates He called them to guard. Everything will be evaluated. Not for condemnation, because the blood of Jesus covers that, but for accountability. For the giving of an account.

This gate is not meant to create fear. It's meant to create maturity.

The Inspection Gate is why the entire roadmap matters. It's why the valley was necessary. It's why the Dung Gate couldn't be skipped. It's why the Fountain Gate was essential. It's why the Water Gate had to be walked through. Because without maturity and without divine purpose, you won't be ready for this final inspection. Not ready in the sense of being condemned, but ready in the sense of having something to show. Ready in the sense of having been faithful with what God gave you. Ready in the sense of having stood in the gap when God was looking for someone to stand there.

The Inspection Gate asks one question of every watchman: did you stay on the wall?

Think about what Jesus said in Matthew 16:19. "Whatever you bind on earth shall be bound in heaven, and whatever you loose on earth shall be loosed in heaven." Those words bind and loose are contractual. Legal. When you bind something in the spirit, you're making a spiritual contract that has legal standing in heaven. When you loose something, it cannot be bound. You're not just praying. You're issuing decrees that carry the weight of heaven's government behind them. And one day, at the Inspection Gate, those decrees will be part of the account you give.

What did you bind? What did you loose? What did you decree over your family that changed the trajectory of their lives? What did you stand against in the spirit that never got through the gate because you were there? What did you pray for your church that kept division from taking root? What did you intercede for your city that shifted the spiritual atmosphere? These aren't small things. They're the substance of a watchman's account before God.

There's something else about the Inspection Gate that's critical for intercessors to understand. Jesus, in Luke 22:31-32, told Simon Peter that Satan had demanded a trial against him. The word translated "asked" in that passage literally means to demand a legal proceeding. Satan stood before the throne of God and used Peter's failures as legal evidence to gain a right to destroy him. And what did Jesus do? He didn't just pray a hopeful prayer. He made a righteous decree. He declared Peter righteous, innocent, and forgiven on the basis of the cross. That's legislative intercession. That's what Jesus did as our High Priest and Advocate.

And that's exactly what you're called to do for the people in your sphere.

When the enemy brings a case against someone you're praying for, when he uses their failures and their past as legal grounds to destroy them, you don't just ask God to help them. You stand before the courts of heaven and you make a righteous decree. You say, "On the basis of the blood of Jesus Christ, this person is righteous, innocent, and forgiven. The enemy has no legal right to what he's claiming. I bind his accusation right now in the name of Jesus, and I loose the full freedom that the cross purchased over this person's life." That's a spiritual contract. That's a legal decree. And it has binding authority in the spirit realm.

The Inspection Gate also carries a word of mercy that's easy to miss. God's goal has never been to catch believers failing. His goal is to save souls for eternity. There are times when God, in His mercy, will allow a person to go through a complete dismantling of everything they've built, not to punish them, but to save their soul from a path that was leading them away from Him. He'll strip away every false thing, every self-built structure, every deception they were operating under, brick by brick, until they have nothing left but Him. That's not judgment. That's mercy. Because God doesn't care about preserving your comfort in this age. He cares about your soul being ready for eternity. The Inspection Gate is the moment when all of that becomes clear.

This should shape how you intercede for people who seem to be losing everything. When you see someone in your sphere going through a complete collapse, when everything they built seems to be falling apart, don't just pray for restoration of what they had. Pray first for the salvation of their soul. Pray that God's mercy does its full work. Pray that whatever needs to come down comes down, and that what God is building in its place is something that will stand at the Inspection Gate. That kind of intercession requires maturity. It requires the ability to see past the immediate pain to the eternal purpose. It requires a watchman who has been through enough valleys of their own to trust that God knows what He's doing even when it looks like destruction.

Living with integrity in the context of the Inspection Gate means that your prayer life and your daily life are the same thing. You can't stand in the gap in the prayer room and then live outside of it in ways that contradict what you're decreeing. The Inspection Gate will evaluate both. It will look at the prayers you prayed and the life you lived. It will look at whether you stayed on the wall when it was hard, whether you kept your post when the spirits of discouragement and slander and confusion came at you, whether you held the line for the people God assigned to you even when you couldn't see any results.

This is what it means to carry the *Shamar* anointing over your family and your city. It's not just a prayer strategy. It's a way of life. It's waking up every morning with the awareness that you've been given a post, a specific territory, a specific group of people, and a specific assignment from God. And it's going to bed every night having stayed in that post, having prayed with precision, having decreed with authority, having kept watch over what God entrusted to you. Day after day. Season after season. Until the East Gate opens and the King comes through.

That's the life the Inspection Gate is evaluating. Not perfection. Faithfulness. Not the absence of valleys. The willingness to go through them and come out the other side still standing. Not the absence of attacks from the enemy. The decision to stay on the wall when all three spirits came at you and tried to pull you off.

Did you stay?

That's the question of the Inspection Gate. And the answer is being written right now, in every prayer you pray, every decree you issue, every time you choose to stay in your place of intercession when everything in you wants to quit. The account you'll give one day is being built today, one prayer at a time, one gate at a time, one person at a time.

Your Next Move

This chapter closed the full roadmap. From the Sheep Gate to the Inspection Gate, the entire cycle now has a context that's bigger than personal growth. It's connected to the return of a King and the giving of an account before a sovereign God. That's the weight every watchman needs to carry into their prayer life starting today.

Here are four specific actions to take right now.

First, evaluate your current activities against your eternal purpose. Take thirty minutes this week to sit before God with a blank page and write down everything you're currently doing in your prayer life and your ministry. Then ask one question about each item: does this push people closer to readiness for the return of Christ? Not just closer to a better life. Closer to eternal readiness. If something on your list doesn't connect to that goal in any clear way, ask God whether it belongs in your current assignment. This isn't about cutting everything down. It's about making sure your *Shamar* call is anchored in the right ultimate goal.

Second, add the East Gate to your daily prayer time. Every single day, before you pray anything else, speak these words out loud: "Lord, I stand at my post today with the awareness that you are coming back. I pray with urgency for the people in my sphere. Push them through the cycle toward readiness. Let nothing the enemy has planned for them succeed while I am standing in the gap." Thirty seconds. Every day. It repositions everything that follows.

Third, pray the Inspection Gate prayer over yourself once a week. On a specific day, preferably the same day each week, sit before God and pray this: "God, I give you access to evaluate my post this week. Show me where I've been faithful and where I've drifted. Show me if I've been pulled off the wall by discouragement, slander, or confusion. I want to stand before the Inspection Gate one day having stayed in my place. Correct me now so I can finish well." Write down whatever He shows you. Act on it the same day.

Fourth, identify one person in your sphere who is not yet walking in their divine purpose and commit to praying them through the Water Gate for the next thirty days. One person. Specific. Named. Pray the four prayer points from the first section of this chapter over them every day for thirty days. Decree that the promises God wrote over their life come alive in this season. Decree that fear and confusion are broken off their assignment. Decree that the right doors open at the right time. Thirty days of targeted, consistent, faith-filled intercession over one person. That's not a small commitment. But it's exactly the kind of faithfulness that the Inspection Gate is looking for.

The *Shamar* anointing over your family and your city is built in the daily choices. Stay on the wall. Keep the East Gate in your spirit. Live like the Inspection Gate is real. And pray the people God gave you all the way through the cycle, gate by gate, until the King comes back through the East.

Activation & Reflection

---

1. How does understanding the end-times assignment of watchmen change the urgency of your prayer life?

____

____

____

____

2. In what way does the reality of standing before God's judgment seat motivate or reshape your intercession?

____

____

____

____

3. Who in your sphere of influence needs an intercessor right now — someone standing in the gap before their time runs out?

____

____

____

____

4. How has God shown you specific purposes tied to your intercessory assignment that connect to His eternal plan?

5. What would it look like for you to pray with true eschatological urgency — as if every prayer session could be the last before the return of Christ?

A Prayer of Urgent Intercession

Lord of Hosts, with eternity in view, I take my intercessory post more seriously than ever. I intercede for the lost and the wandering. I pray for the sleeping Church to awaken. I ask for more time — and the wisdom to use it well. May every prayer I offer be counted as faithful service before Your throne. Keep my eyes fixed on what matters eternally. In Jesus' name, Amen.

CHAPTER 5

Defining Your Spiritual Metron

Locating Your Sphere of Authority

There's a word you need to write down and understand before you take another step in your prayer life. That word is *metron*. It's a Greek word that means your specific sphere of spiritual influence. It's the territory God has assigned to you in the spirit. It's the boundary line around the people and the places where your prayers carry the most legal weight. And until you understand it, you'll keep showing up to spiritual battles where your authority doesn't reach, wondering why nothing is moving, wondering why God seems silent, wondering why you're exhausted but not producing results.

The *metron* is not about how anointed you are. It's not about how long you've been saved or how many hours you've spent in prayer. It's about assignment. It's about where God has specifically placed you and the relational authority that placement gives you in the spirit. Think about what Acts 1:8 says: Jerusalem, Judea, Samaria, and the ends of the earth. Those aren't just geographical locations. They're metrons. They're concentric circles of spiritual influence, each one requiring a specific kind of authority to operate in effectively.

James had the *metron* of Jerusalem. That was his assigned sphere. His relational authority in that city was so recognized in the spirit that even Paul, who carried a global calling, understood he had to honor James's jurisdiction when he came to Jerusalem. Paul didn't walk in and start making decrees over the city as if James wasn't there. He met with the apostle of Jerusalem first. He honored the *metron*. That's not a small detail. That's a pattern for how authority works in the kingdom of God.

Your *metron* right now might be your household. It might be the small group you lead. It might be your local church, your workplace, or your neighborhood. It might be a combination of all of those. The size doesn't matter at this stage. What matters is that you locate it accurately. Because a watchman who doesn't know their assigned territory will do one of two things. They'll either pray too small, staying so focused on themselves that they never carry the burden for the people God actually assigned to them. Or they'll pray too large, pushing into regions and situations where they have no relational authority, fighting battles they weren't sent to fight, and coming home spiritually bruised because the enemy had every right to push back.

Both of those mistakes are costly. And both of them are avoidable once you understand the *metron*.

So here's your first specific action. Take a blank piece of paper right now and draw three circles, one inside the other like a target. In the smallest inner circle, write the names of the people closest to you, your spouse, your children, the people who live under your roof. These are the people you have the deepest relational authority over in the spirit. In the middle circle, write your church community, your close friendships, your workplace relationships, the people you have consistent, meaningful contact with. In the outer circle, write your city or region, the broader territory where God has placed you geographically and where your prayers carry some level of influence because of your assignment there. Now look at what you've drawn. That's your current *metron*. That's the territory God has given you legal standing to pray over with authority. Start there. Stay there. And watch what happens when your prayers are aimed at the right target.

Your influence in the spirit is tied directly to your relational authority in the natural. You can't effectively persuade God on behalf of a territory you have no relationship with and no assignment in. That's not a limitation of God's power. It's a reflection of how He designed authority to work. He built the kingdom on relationship, not on volume. The person who prays with deep relational authority over five people will see more movement than the person who shouts loud prayers over a thousand people they've never met. Depth beats breadth every time when it comes to the *metron*.

Authority Through Relationship

One of the most common misunderstandings in the body of Christ is the idea that spiritual authority comes from a title. People think that if they can get a certain position in a church, if they can get someone to call them prophet or apostle or intercessor, then they'll have authority in the spirit. But that's not how it works. Titles don't give you authority. Relationship does. Alignment does. The willingness to be accountable to those God has placed over you does. Authority in the spirit is always built from the inside out, not from the outside in.

Paul made this clear in his own life. He said, "I am an apostle, but I am an apostle to you who accept me as one." His authority wasn't self-declared and universally applicable. It was relational and contextual. It was real in the places where relationship had been built and where his assignment had been recognized. Outside of those places, he still operated with wisdom and grace, but he understood that the weight of his apostolic authority was most concentrated in the spheres where God had specifically sent him.

That same principle applies to you as an intercessor and watchman. Your relational authority in your home is different from your relational authority in your church, which is different from your relational authority in your city. Each level requires a different kind of standing. And that standing is built through faithfulness, through consistency, through the willingness to serve the vision of those God has placed over you, and through the depth of relationship you've cultivated with the people in your sphere.

Think about what this means practically. In your home, you have a level of spiritual authority that nobody else on earth has over those specific people. You've been placed there by God. You share life with them. You know their struggles, their fears, their patterns. That intimacy gives you a depth of intercessory authority that a stranger praying for them from across the country simply doesn't carry. When you pray for your children, you're not just a believer asking God to help somebody. You're the watchman God assigned to that household, standing in the gap with relational authority that carries legal weight in the spirit.

In your local church, your authority is built through your relationship with the vision and the leadership God has placed there. This is where many intercessors miss it. They show up, they pray hard, they feel strong spiritual impressions, but they haven't submitted to the covering of the house. They haven't aligned their hearts with the vision of the pastor or the apostle. And because of that misalignment, their prayers over the church carry less weight than they could. Authority in a house comes through relationship with the house. It comes through serving the vision, honoring the leadership, and allowing your heart to be knit to the people God has placed you with.

Your pastor or spiritual leader isn't just a person you listen to on Sundays. They're a spiritual covering. And when you genuinely align yourself under that covering, something happens in the spirit. Their grace becomes your grace. Their assignment extends to include you. The battles they're fighting become battles you have legal standing to intercede in, because you're under the same authority, serving the same vision, carrying the same burden. That's not spiritual control. That's kingdom order. And kingdom order is what gives intercession its power.

Here's the specific practice for identifying your relational authority in each circle of your *metron*. For your home: write down each person's name and next to it, write one specific spiritual burden you carry for them. Not a general concern. A specific one. The thing that wakes you up at night for them. The pattern you've seen in their life that you know needs prayer. That burden is evidence of your relational authority. God gave you that burden because He gave you that assignment. For your church: write down the vision of your local church as you understand it. If you can't write it in one or two sentences, you need to get closer to the leadership until you can. Then ask yourself honestly: am I serving this vision with my time, my prayer, and my heart? If the answer is yes, your intercessory authority in that house is real and active. If the answer is no, that's your next step before you pray for the church at a watchman level. For your city: write down one specific thing God has consistently laid on your heart about your city. One pattern, one need, one spiritual dynamic that you keep coming back to. That's the thread of your *metron* in your city. Pull on it. Pray into it. That's where your city-level authority is concentrated.

Spiritual authority isn't complicated. It's relational. It's built through love, through faithfulness, through the willingness to stay connected to the people and the vision God has assigned to you even when it's hard. And when that foundation is in place, your prayers carry a weight that moves things in the spirit in a way that no amount of volume or intensity can replace.

The Danger of Stepping Outside Your Metron

There's a story in Acts 19 that every intercessor and watchman needs to sit with for a long time. The seven sons of Sceva saw Paul casting out demons in the name of Jesus. They thought they could do the same thing. They walked up to a man with an evil spirit and said, "We command you in the name of Jesus whom Paul preaches." The demon's response is one of the most sobering moments in the New Testament. The evil spirit answered and said, "Jesus I know, and Paul I know, but who are you?" And then the man with the evil spirit jumped on them, overpowered them all, and they fled out of the house naked and wounded.

They tried to operate outside their *metron*. They had no relational authority with Jesus. They had no assignment from God. They had no covering, no submission, no alignment. And the spirit world knew it. The demons recognized it. And the consequence was immediate and physical.

That's not just a Bible story. That's a warning for right now.

When you push into spiritual warfare in a region where you have no assignment, no relational authority, and no covering, you don't just fail to get results. You expose yourself to spiritual backlash. Demons are rebellious by nature. They're assigned to specific territories. And when you walk into their region without being sent and without proper authority, they don't just ignore you. They push back. They follow you back to your region. They attack the things closest to you, your family, your health, your mind, the people in your actual *metron* who are now unguarded because you went somewhere you weren't supposed to go.

The key question before any significant act of spiritual warfare is not "do I feel called to this?" Feelings can be genuine and still be premature. The right questions are three. First: am I properly aligned with Christ right now? Is there anything between me and God that needs to be dealt with before I step into this? Second: am I properly covered? Is there a spiritual authority in my life who knows what I'm doing and has released me to do it? Third: am I invited or sent? Has God specifically directed me to this territory, or am I going because I feel zealous and want to do something significant?

All three questions need a clear yes before you move.

Being invited means someone with authority in that region has asked you to come and pray. Being sent means

God has specifically directed you to go, and that sending has been confirmed through your spiritual covering. Both of these things matter. If you're invited but not sent, you might be going for the wrong reasons. If you feel sent but no one in authority over you has confirmed it, slow down. Spiritual authority has a proper flow in the kingdom. God works through order. And when you honor that order, the grace of your covering goes with you. When you bypass it, you go alone. And going alone into high-level spiritual warfare is one of the most dangerous things a watchman can do.

There's also something important to understand about how angels operate in relation to your *metron*. Your angels recognize your sphere of influence. They're assigned to work in agreement with your authority. When you're praying within your *metron*, they can engage. They can fight on your behalf. They can carry your decrees to their intended target. But when you step outside your *metron* without proper authority, your angels aren't authorized to protect you in that territory. The only angels who step outside their ordained boundaries, according to Jude, are angels in rebellion against God. Your angels are not rebellious. They operate within divine order. And if you push past your boundaries, you're pushing past theirs too.

This doesn't mean you never pray for things beyond your immediate circle. You can intercede for nations. You can pray for people you've never met. But there's a difference between praying for something and engaging in direct spiritual warfare against principalities in a region where you have no assignment. One is intercession. The other is confrontation. And confrontation requires jurisdiction. Before you confront a principality over a city or a region, ask yourself honestly: has God sent me here? Do I have the covering of someone with apostolic authority over this territory? Have I been invited by the spiritual authority of this land? If the answer to those questions isn't a clear yes, then your assignment is to pray and intercede, not to confront and command.

The protection that comes from staying within your *metron* isn't a restriction. It's a grace. God isn't limiting you by defining your boundaries. He's protecting you. He's keeping you in the place where your prayers carry the most weight and where the covering over you can keep you safe. A lot of people feel like boundaries in the spirit are about control. They're not. They're about protection. And a watchman who understands this doesn't chafe against the boundaries of their *metron*. They're grateful for them. Because they know what it costs to step outside them without authorization.

Stay in your lane. Guard your post. Be invited or be sent. And when you're not sure which one applies, stay home and pray until you are sure. That's not timidity. That's wisdom. And wisdom keeps you effective for the long haul.

Expanding Your Influence

Your current *metron* is not your final *metron*. God doesn't assign you a sphere of influence and then leave it the same size forever. The kingdom is designed to expand. Influence is designed to grow. And the path from where you are now to where God wants to take you runs through two specific things: faithfulness in your current assignment and connection to apostolic grace.

Faithfulness is the foundation. You don't get a larger *metron* by asking for one. You get it by being trustworthy with the one you already have. When God sees that you've been a faithful watchman over your household, that you've stayed at your post even when it was hard, that you've prayed your family through the cycle with consistency and authority, that's when He begins to expand the boundary. When He sees that you've served the vision of your local church with your whole heart, that you've aligned yourself under the covering of your spiritual authority, that you've been faithful to intercede for the house even when nobody knew you were doing it, that's when the circle gets bigger. Promotion in the spirit works the same way it does in the natural. You prove yourself with what you have before you're trusted with more.

Luke 16:10 says it plainly: "Whoever can be trusted with very little can also be trusted with much." That's the law of the *metron*. The person who is faithful over five names on their prayer list will eventually be given fifty. The person who guards their household with *Shamar* authority will eventually be given a church to guard. The person who prays faithfully for their city will eventually be given a region. But it doesn't happen out of order. It happens as the fruit of faithfulness in the current assignment, one level at a time.

The second key to expanding your *metron* is connection to apostolic grace. This is where many intercessors miss a significant acceleration in their calling. An apostle is a sent one. Someone God has placed an anointing on to think beyond the local, to carry a vision that extends to nations, to release others into assignments that go further than they could reach on their own. When you connect your heart to an apostle, something transfers. Paul told Timothy to stir up the gift that was imparted when Paul laid hands on him. Timothy wasn't just receiving prayer. He was receiving an apostolic grace that expanded his capacity and his reach. Paul even told the churches that Timothy would operate so much like Paul that it would seem as if Paul himself had been there. That's the power of apostolic connection. My assignment becomes your assignment. My grace becomes your grace. My reach extends to include you.

This is why spiritual covering isn't just about protection. It's about expansion. When you're genuinely connected to an apostolic grace, the ceiling on your *metron* rises. You start thinking in terms of nations instead of just neighborhoods. You start praying with the weight of a vision that's bigger than your personal sphere. And as you serve that vision faithfully, as you pour yourself into it with your prayers and your time and your heart, your own influence begins to grow to match the size of what you're connected to. You can't stay small when you're connected to something large and you're genuinely serving it from the heart.

There's a practical sequence to expanding your *metron* that you need to follow. It has four steps. Step one: be faithful where you are right now. Don't despise the current size of your sphere. Guard it with everything you have. Pray over every name in your inner circle with the same urgency and authority you'd want to bring to a city. Step two: serve the vision of your local church or apostolic covering with your whole heart. Not for what you can get from it. Not to be seen or recognized. But because you've genuinely aligned your heart with what God is building through that house. Step three: ask your spiritual covering to release you into the next level when the time is right. Don't assume. Don't push. Ask. And let them confirm the timing. Step four: when the door opens to a larger sphere, carry the same faithfulness that built your current one. Don't change your posture just because your platform got bigger. The watchman who guards a household and the watchman who guards a city are the same person with the same character. The territory is different. The faithfulness is identical.

There are also biblical metrons that every believer carries regardless of their personal assignment. Israel is one of them. Genesis 12:3 says that God will bless those who bless Israel and curse those who curse it. That's a covenant *metron*. Every believer has some level of spiritual authority to pray for the peace of Jerusalem and for the fulfillment of God's purposes in that land. You don't need a special apostolic assignment to intercede for Israel. You need a covenant understanding of why God's heart is still turned toward that nation and what your prayers accomplish in that context. Pray for Israel regularly. It's not optional for a watchman who understands covenant. It's part of the foundation.

Your *metron* will grow. It's designed to. But it grows through the same things that built it in the first place: prayer, faithfulness, submission, and connection to the right grace. Stay in that process. Don't rush it. And trust that the God who wrote your assignment before you were born knows exactly how large your sphere is supposed to become and exactly when each expansion is supposed to happen.

Recap and Action Steps

The *metron* is your legal sphere of authority in the spirit. It's the territory where your prayers carry the most weight, where your angels are authorized to work on your behalf, and where your relational authority gives you legal standing before the courts of heaven to intercede with precision and power. It's not about the size of your sphere. It's about the faithfulness and the authority you bring to whatever size God has currently assigned to you.

You can't effectively fight for territory where you have no assignment. You can't persuade God on behalf of people you have no relationship with at the same level you can for those He's specifically placed in your care. You can't confront principalities in regions where you haven't been sent without exposing yourself to spiritual backlash. And you can't expand your influence by bypassing the process of faithfulness in your current assignment. All of these truths work together to form one clear picture: know your *metron*, stay in it, guard it with everything you have, and trust God to expand it in His timing.

Here are your action steps for this chapter. They're specific. Do them in order.

First, draw your *metron* map today. Get a blank piece of paper and draw the three circles described in the first section of this chapter. Fill in each circle with the specific names and relationships that belong there. Don't overthink it. You know who God has placed in your sphere. Write their names down. That map is now your primary prayer target. Every day this week, pray over at least one person from each circle with specific, targeted intercession based on where they are in the Nehemiah roadmap.

Second, write down your relational authority in three areas. Your home, your church, and your city. For each one, write one sentence that describes your specific assignment in that sphere. For example: "In my home, I am the watchman assigned to guard my children's minds and my marriage from spiritual attack." "In my church, I am the intercessor assigned to pray for the vision of this house and the protection of the leadership." "In my city, I carry a burden for the youth and I pray specifically against the spirit of addiction that's targeting that generation." These aren't just nice statements. They're declarations of assignment. Speak them out loud. They anchor you to your post.

Third, ask God one direct question this week in a dedicated listening prayer time. Set aside at least thirty minutes, sit before Him in silence, and ask: "God, where are the exact boundaries of my current assignment? Show me where my authority reaches and where it ends." Write down everything He shows you. This isn't a one-time exercise. It's the beginning of a practice of regularly checking in with God about the shape of your *metron*, because as you grow in faithfulness, the boundaries will shift.

Fourth, identify your apostolic covering and evaluate your alignment with it. Who is the spiritual authority God has placed over your life? Are you genuinely serving their vision? Are you submitted to their covering in a real, active way? If the answer is yes, thank God for that covering and ask Him to show you how to serve it more effectively. If the answer is no, or if you don't have a clear covering, make finding and aligning with one your priority before you attempt any high-level spiritual warfare. You need a tree to rest under. You need someone of higher authority whose grace can cover your battles. Don't go into the fight uncovered.

The *Shamar* anointing over your family and your city is built on the foundation of a clearly defined *metron*. When you know where you're assigned, you stop wasting energy on battles that aren't yours and you pour everything you have into the ones that are. That's when your prayers stop feeling like they're bouncing off the ceiling and start feeling like they're landing exactly where they're supposed to. That's when you stop being frustrated in intercession and start being effective. Know your sphere. Guard it. And let God expand it in His time.

Activation & Reflection

---

1. How would you describe your spiritual metron — the specific sphere of authority and influence God has assigned to you?

____

____

____

____

2. What happens when you pray outside your assigned metron? Have you witnessed the consequences of overreaching in prayer?

____

____

____

____

3. What unique gifts, experiences, and relationships define the boundaries of your spiritual jurisdiction?

____

____

____

____

4. How can you honor another person's metron while still fulfilling your own intercessory assignment faithfully?

____

____

____

____

5. Write out a specific declaration of your metron — the people, places, and purposes God has called you to cover in prayer.

____

____

____

____

A Prayer of Alignment

Father, I submit to the boundaries of my spiritual metron. Show me clearly the spheres You have assigned to me, and give me the wisdom to remain within my appointed jurisdiction. I renounce the temptation to overreach and the cowardice to underperform. Expand my metron as You see fit and give me the authority to operate fully within it. I will faithfully steward what You have given me. In Jesus' name, Amen.

CHAPTER 6

The Power of Spiritual Covering

Resting Under the Tree of Authority

There's a picture that captures what spiritual covering actually looks like better than almost any theological explanation ever could. Imagine a large tree on a hot day. Its branches spread wide. Its shade reaches far. And underneath it, a person is resting. Not straining. Not fighting. Not anxious about what's happening in the open field beyond the shade. Just resting. Because someone bigger, someone with more reach, someone with deeper roots, is handling what they can't handle on their own.

That's covering.

It sounds simple. But most believers have never fully experienced it because they've never fully submitted to it. And the reason they haven't submitted to it is the same reason every time. Pride. Not always the loud, obvious kind. Sometimes it's the quiet kind. The kind that says, "I can hear God for myself." The kind that says, "I don't need someone over me." The kind that mistakes independence for spiritual maturity and ends up exposed to battles it was never equipped to fight alone.

The only people who resist submission are people who don't understand what it's actually offering them. Submission to a spiritual covering isn't a restriction on your freedom. It's protection over your assignment. It's not God putting a ceiling over you. It's God putting a shield around you. The moment you understand that distinction, everything about how you relate to spiritual authority changes.

Think about what Jesus said in Luke 9:58. He said the foxes have holes and the birds have nests, but the Son of Man has nowhere to lay His head. That wasn't just a statement about homelessness. It was a statement about what was coming. Jesus could see the cross ahead of Him. He knew what He was walking into. And He understood that no one on earth could shelter Him from it. Only the Father could carry that weight. But when Peter stumbled, when Satan demanded a trial against him and the enemy was positioning to sift him like wheat, Jesus didn't leave Peter to fight it alone. He said, "I have prayed for you." That's covering. That's someone of higher authority stepping into the gap and handling what you couldn't handle on your own.

Peter ran under the tree. And the tree held.

The same principle is what God designed for every watchman and intercessor. You're not supposed to carry the full weight of your assignment in isolation. You're designed to operate under a covering, under someone whose *metron* is larger than yours, whose angels go further than yours, whose sacrifice and intercession create a canopy that extends over your life and your work. When you're under that covering, you can rest. Not because the battle isn't real, but because someone of higher authority is already engaged in the fight at a level you haven't yet been released to.

This is why the sons of Sceva story in Acts 19 matters so much for watchmen. They tried to operate without covering. They had no alignment with Christ. They had no submission to apostolic authority. They walked into a confrontation with a demonic spirit and said, "We command you in the name of Jesus whom Paul preaches." The demon looked at them and said, "Jesus I know, and Paul I know, but who are you?" And then it attacked them. They ran out of that house naked and wounded. Not because the name of Jesus wasn't powerful. But because they had no legal standing to use it. They weren't under covering. They weren't under authority. And the spirit world knew it.

Had those men been submitted to Paul, had they been genuinely aligned under his apostolic covering, that demon couldn't have said what it said. It would have looked at them and seen Paul's grace on them. It would have recognized the authority of their covering. And it would have had to respond accordingly. That's not a small thing. That's the difference between spiritual effectiveness and spiritual exposure. And it comes down entirely to whether you're under the tree or standing in the open field on your own.

Now here's what covering looks like in a practical sense for a watchman. Think about a hypothetical scenario. Consider a woman named Priya, a 33-year-old intercessor who has been praying for her city for two years. She's gifted. She feels things deeply in the spirit. She's been waking up at three in the morning with burdens she can't explain. But she's been doing all of this in isolation, without connecting to a local church in any meaningful way, without submitting to any spiritual authority, without telling anyone what she's praying or why. She feels free. Uncontrolled. Able to go wherever she feels led. But over time, something starts to happen. She gets spiritually tired in a way that rest doesn't fix. She starts having confusion about her assignment. She starts doubting what God told her. She picks up spiritual weight she can't identify and can't shake. What Priya is experiencing isn't a failure of faith. It's the consequence of operating without a covering. She's been standing in the open field, carrying battles that were always meant to be fought from under the shade of a tree. The moment Priya connects to an apostolic covering, submits her assignment to that authority, and begins to pray from within that alignment, the confusion lifts. The weight becomes manageable. The battles she's been losing start to turn. Not because she prayed harder. But because she finally got under the tree.

Here's what you need to do specifically to walk in the protection of spiritual covering. First, identify who your covering is right now. Not who you wish it was. Who God has actually placed over your life in this season. This is the pastor, the apostle, the spiritual father or mother who carries a genuine assignment over the territory where you live and serve. If you can't name that person, finding them is your first priority before you attempt any serious level of spiritual warfare. You can't fight effectively from an uncovered position.

Second, submit your assignment to them. This doesn't mean you need their permission for every prayer you pray. It means you bring your watchman call under the umbrella of their vision and their authority. Tell them what you're carrying. Ask them to pray over you. Ask them to release you into what God has put on your heart. When they do, their grace goes with you. Their angels extend to cover you. The battles you face in your assignment now have a higher authority engaged on your behalf. That's not dependency. That's kingdom order working exactly the way God designed it.

Third, pray for your covering specifically and consistently. Not just a general "God bless my pastor" prayer. Targeted intercession for the person or people who carry authority over your life. Pray for their health. Pray for their clarity of vision. Pray for their protection from the three spirits that attack every person in a place of spiritual authority. Pray that discouragement doesn't pull them off their wall. Pray that slander doesn't discredit them before the people they're called to lead. Pray that confusion doesn't cloud their assignment. A watchman who prays for their covering is building something in the spirit that protects both of them. Your prayers over your covering strengthen the tree you're resting under. And a stronger tree provides better shade.

Fourth, ask God to show you any area of pride that's been preventing you from fully resting under your covering. This is the most important step and the one most people skip. Pride doesn't always feel like pride. Sometimes it feels like discernment. Sometimes it feels like independence. Sometimes it feels like you're just being careful. But if there's a part of you that resists accountability, resists being known by a spiritual authority, resists having someone speak into your assignment, that's worth examining before God. Sit with Him in silence and ask directly: "Is there pride in me that's keeping me from fully receiving the protection you've designed for this season?" Write down what He shows you. Then bring it to the Dung Gate and drop it off. Because pride at the gate of your covering will cost you more than you realize.

The enemy's strategy against watchmen isn't always a frontal attack. Sometimes it's much more subtle. He works to isolate. He works to convince you that you're too spiritually advanced to need oversight. He works to create small offenses between you and your covering so that the relationship gets strained and the canopy of protection gets thin. He knows that a watchman without covering is a watchman without backup. And a watchman without backup is a watchman who's one hard battle away from being overwhelmed.

Don't let him isolate you. Get under the tree. Stay there. And rest in the protection that God designed for every person carrying the *Shamar* call.

The Apostolic Impartation

Covering isn't just about protection. That's the part most people understand, at least in theory. But there's another dimension of spiritual covering that most believers never fully access, and it's the one that can accelerate your calling in ways that years of personal effort alone never could. That dimension is impartation. The transfer of grace, anointing, and apostolic assignment that flows from a spiritual father or mother to someone genuinely connected to them in the spirit.

Paul said it plainly to Timothy. "Stir up the gift that was imparted to you when I laid my hands on you." That's 2 Timothy 1:6. Timothy didn't work for everything he carried. He received some of it. Paul laid hands on him and something transferred. Not a feeling. Not just an emotional moment. An actual grace. An actual assignment. An actual dimension of spiritual authority that Timothy didn't have before that moment. And Paul expected Timothy to steward it, to stir it up, to keep it active and burning.

Paul even told the churches something remarkable about Timothy. He said, when Timothy comes to you, you'll think I've been there myself. Because of how he operates. Think about what that means. Timothy walked into a room and people encountered the same spirit, the same grace, the same apostolic weight that they would have encountered if Paul himself had walked in. Not because Timothy was Paul. But because Timothy was genuinely connected to Paul's assignment in the spirit. His sacrifice became Timothy's sacrifice. His reach became Timothy's reach. His grace became Timothy's grace. That's the power of apostolic impartation. You don't have to build everything from scratch when you're genuinely connected to someone who has already built it through their own obedience, their own sacrifice, their own years of faithfulness before God.

This is one of the most underutilized truths in the body of Christ. Believers spend years trying to develop in the spirit what they could receive through genuine connection to apostolic grace. They fast and pray and work hard, which are all right and necessary things. But they do all of it disconnected from the grace that God has already deposited in the apostolic leaders He placed in their lives. And so they build slowly, painfully, from zero, when God designed for them to start from a much higher place because of the grace available through their covering.

When you get connected to grace, your life starts now. Not five years from now. Not after you've figured everything out on your own. Now. Because the grace you're connecting to has already been tested, already been proven, already been forged through the sacrifice and the faithfulness of the person who carries it. You don't have to repeat every lesson they learned. You don't have to make every mistake they made. You step into an inheritance that their obedience built, and you carry it further from the place where they left off.

But here's the critical thing about impartation that most people miss. It doesn't transfer through proximity. You can sit in the same room as an apostle every Sunday for ten years and receive almost nothing if your heart isn't connected. Grace is received through the heart, not just the ears. The woman in the hypothetical example from the source of this teaching received a prophetic word that unlocked two and a half years of blocked finances. She didn't receive it the moment it was spoken from the platform. She received it the moment her heart connected to it, the moment she ran to the altar and let the word land in her spirit rather than just her mind. The word was the same. The timing of the breakthrough was different. Because grace connects through the heart.

That means your posture toward your apostolic covering determines how much of what they carry actually transfers to you. If you sit under an anointed leader with a critical spirit, analyzing everything they say, comparing them to other leaders, holding them at arm's length because of past hurt or pride, you'll walk out of that room with nothing. The anointing passed right over you because your heart was closed. But if you sit under that same leader with a genuinely open, submitted, hungry heart, if you receive what they carry as a gift from God to your specific assignment, if you let their sacrifice become your sacrifice in the spirit, you'll walk out of that room carrying something you didn't walk in with.

That's impartation. And it's available to you every time you're in the presence of someone God has assigned to pour into your life.

So here's what you need to do to actively receive apostolic impartation rather than just being around it. The first thing is to connect with your heart before you connect with your ears. Before you sit under your covering, before you enter a service or a meeting where your spiritual authority will be ministering, take five minutes to prepare your heart. Pray something like this: "God, I'm coming to receive today. I'm not coming to evaluate or analyze. I'm coming with my heart open to receive whatever you want to transfer through this vessel. Let their grace become my grace. Let their assignment extend to include me. I receive it now in the name of Jesus." That's not a ritual. That's a spiritual positioning that opens the channel for impartation to flow.

The second thing is to stir up what's already been imparted. Paul told Timothy to stir up the gift. That word "stir" carries the idea of fanning a flame that's been allowed to die down. Impartation doesn't maintain itself automatically. It requires your active participation. You stir it up through prayer, through use, through stepping out in faith to operate in the grace you received. If your covering laid hands on you and released you into an assignment, you stir that up by actually doing the assignment. If they spoke a prophetic word over your prayer life, you stir that up by praying with the authority that word released. Impartation that isn't stirred up will fade. Impartation that's actively stewarded will grow.

The third thing is to honor the sacrifice behind the grace. Timothy didn't just receive an anointing. He received the fruit of Paul's imprisonment, Paul's beatings, Paul's years of suffering for the gospel. That sacrifice was embedded in the grace. And when Timothy carried that grace, he was carrying the weight of everything Paul went through to build it. That's not a small thing to receive. And it demands a certain kind of honor. Not honor as in flattery or performance. Honor as in genuine reverence for what it cost the person to carry what they're now releasing to you. When you understand the sacrifice behind the grace of your covering, you stop treating their impartation casually. You steward it with the seriousness it deserves. Because you know it was purchased at a price.

There's also something powerful that happens in the spirit when you're genuinely connected to apostolic grace and you're operating in your *metron*. Your covering's angels extend to cover your assignment. When a leader with a *metron* that reaches nations sends you into a specific territory or releases you into a specific assignment, their angels go with you. Not because of you. Because of the assignment of Christ that flows through the apostolic grace you're connected to. That's why being properly sent matters so much. Not just feeling called. Being sent. Being released by someone with the authority to release you. Because when you're sent, you don't go alone. You go carrying the grace of the one who sent you. And that grace has angels attached to it that reach further than your own *metron* currently does.

Think about what this means for your prayer life specifically. If you're connected to an apostle or a spiritual leader who carries a burden for nations, your intercession for your local territory is now backed by a grace that thinks globally. Your prayers for your household carry the weight of an apostolic assignment that's bigger than your household. You're praying from inside a larger grace than you built on your own. And that makes your intercession more effective, more authoritative, and more far-reaching than it would be if you were standing alone.

This is why the *Shamar* anointing isn't meant to be carried in isolation. It's designed to flow within a structure of covering and impartation. You guard your territory. You stand in the gap for the people God assigned to you. But you do it under the canopy of an apostolic grace that extends above and beyond your personal sphere. You do it as someone who has been sent, not just someone who showed up. You do it carrying the sacrifice of your covering as part of your own spiritual inheritance. And when you operate from that place, the enemy isn't just dealing with you. He's dealing with you and everything that's behind you.

That's a very different fight than the one he's used to winning.

Moving Forward: What to Do With This Chapter

Everything in this chapter points to one truth that runs through the entire *Shamar* call. You were not designed to carry this alone. The guardian anointing over your family and your city is most powerful when it's operating within the structure God designed for it, under covering, connected to apostolic grace, submitted to the authority He placed in your life for this season.

Here are four specific actions to take before you move to the next chapter. Do them in order. Each one builds on the one before it.

The first action is to identify your spiritual covering by name before you do anything else. Not a general idea of church membership. A specific person. The one God has placed in spiritual authority over your life right now. Write their name down. If you genuinely don't have one, write this at the top of your page: "Finding my covering is my first assignment." Then ask God to show you specifically who that person is and where they're located. Don't move past this step until it's answered. Everything else in this chapter depends on it.

The second action is to pray for your covering for seven consecutive days using this specific framework. Day one, pray for their physical health and strength. Day two, pray for their clarity of vision and their ability to hear God clearly. Day three, pray against the spirit of discouragement that targets leaders in high-level assignment. Day four, pray against slander and every attack on their character and credibility. Day five, pray against confusion and every attempt to cloud their thinking about their assignment. Day six, pray for the people in their immediate household, because a leader's home is often the first target of the enemy's strategy against their ministry. Day seven, pray that God expands their *metron* and gives them everything they need to carry the assignment He's placed on them. Write down each day's prayer in a journal. Keep it specific. Keep it targeted. That's not just intercession for them. It's you actively strengthening the tree you're resting under.

The third action is to ask God one direct question about pride in a dedicated fifteen-minute silence before Him this week. Sit down. No phone. No music. No background noise. Ask this question out loud: "God, is there any area of pride in me that's been keeping me from fully resting under the covering you've placed in my life?" Then sit in silence and write down everything that surfaces. Don't defend yourself. Don't explain it away. Just write it down. Whatever He shows you, bring it to Him honestly and release it. Then make one specific change in how you relate to your covering based on what He revealed. Not a vague intention to be more submitted. One specific, observable change. Maybe it's reaching out to your pastor this week and asking them to pray over your watchman assignment. Maybe it's stopping the habit of mentally critiquing their decisions and replacing it with intercession for their wisdom. Whatever it is, make it specific and make it this week.

The fourth action is to prepare your heart to receive impartation the next time you're in the presence of your covering. Before that service, that meeting, or that conversation, pray the five-minute heart-preparation prayer from the second section of this chapter. Come with your heart open. Come expecting that something will transfer. Come ready to receive not just information but grace. And after that time, write down in your journal what you received. What shifted. What you're now carrying that you weren't carrying before. Then ask yourself what it would look like to stir that up this week. What specific act of faith would fan that impartation into flame? Write it down. Do it. Don't let what God deposited in you sit unused.

Covering provides protection. Impartation provides acceleration. Together, they give the *Shamar* watchman access to a corporate grace that goes far beyond what personal effort alone can build. The person who guards their territory from under the canopy of apostolic covering, who receives and stewards the grace imparted to them, who prays for the tree they're resting under with the same urgency they bring to their own assignment, that person doesn't just guard a gate. They carry an authority that the enemy recognizes and respects. Because they're not standing alone. They're standing inside a structure that heaven designed, backed by a grace that their covering's sacrifice built, and covered by angels that their alignment released. That's the full picture of the *Shamar* anointing operating the way God intended it to. Not in isolation. In covering. Under the tree. And from that place, there's nothing the enemy can do that won't eventually be turned back.

Activation & Reflection

---

1. Who has God placed over you as a spiritual covering? How have you honored or neglected that covering?

____

____

____

____

2. Describe a time when operating under proper spiritual authority produced protection or breakthrough in your life.

____

____

____

____

3. Who are you currently called to cover in prayer — and are you doing so faithfully and consistently?

____

____

____

____

4. What is the difference between covering someone in prayer and attempting to control them through prayer?

____

____

____

____

5. How does understanding spiritual covering change the way you approach intercessory prayer for your family or local church?

____

____

____

____

A Prayer Under Covering

Lord, I submit myself under the spiritual covering You have ordained over my life. I honor the leaders and spiritual authorities You have placed above me. Teach me to pray for them rather than criticize them. Help me to faithfully cover those entrusted to me — let no breach in my prayer life leave them exposed. Build a canopy of protection over every person in my care. In Jesus' name, Amen.

CHAPTER 7

Legislative vs. Warfare Prayer

The Highest Form of Intercession

Most Spirit-filled believers have been taught one mode of prayer when things get hard. You raise your voice. You bind the enemy. You declare war. You come in hot and loud and you fight. And there's a place for that. There are absolutely seasons when the Spirit of God calls you to stand up, speak boldly, and push back against the darkness with everything you have. But if that's the only mode you know, you're missing the highest level of what prayer was actually designed to do. And the enemy, frankly, isn't that threatened by noise. He's threatened by legislation.

The highest form of prayer isn't warfare prayer. It's legislative prayer. It's judicial. It operates in the courts of heaven, not just on the battlefield of the earth. And until you understand the difference, you'll keep fighting battles at a level below where they're actually being decided.

Think about how the enemy actually operates. Ephesians 6:12 says we wrestle not against flesh and blood, but against principalities, powers, and rulers of darkness.

Look at those three categories carefully. Principalities, from the word prince. Powers. Rulers. These aren't random evil spirits wandering around causing chaos. These are governmental beings. They operate through rank, through authority, through spiritual legislation. They issue decrees. They write edicts. They make assignments. When the enemy wants to attack your children, he doesn't just show up at your front door with a pitchfork. He goes to a spiritual government and he writes a law. He puts people in positions of natural authority who then make decisions that bind entire generations. The laws that come out of Capitol Hill that leave you shaking your head and wondering how we got here? Those aren't just the result of bad politics. Principalities, powers, and rulers put those people in place. And they work through legislation, through edicts, through spiritual decrees that operate from a governmental seat.

So if your enemy is governmental, your response has to be governmental too.

You can't out-shout a principality. Loud warfare prayer has its place, but principalities don't respond to volume. They respond to legal authority. They respond to decrees issued from a higher court. They respond to edicts that carry the weight of heaven's government behind them. This is why so many intercessors pray hard and long and still don't see the kind of breakthrough they're believing for. They're fighting at the wrong level. They're engaging a governmental enemy with personal warfare prayer when what's needed is a legislative response from the courts of heaven.

Daniel 7:10 gives us a picture of heaven that most believers have read but haven't fully absorbed. It says a river of fire was pouring out from God's presence. Millions of angels ministered to Him. Many millions more stood attending Him. And then it says something that changes everything about how you understand prayer. It says the court began its session and the books were opened. That's not metaphor. That's the governmental reality of heaven. Heaven is a courtroom. God is seated as Judge. The books are open. Cases are being heard. Decrees are being issued. And the question is whether you're showing up to that courtroom with a case or whether you're just making noise outside the building.

Jesus modeled legislative prayer in one of the most significant moments in the Gospels. In Luke 22:31-32, He told Simon Peter something remarkable. He said, "Simon, Simon, Satan has asked for you." That word "asked" in the original language means to demand a legal proceeding. Satan wasn't just attacking Peter. He was standing before the throne of God and demanding a trial. He was using Peter's failures, his weaknesses, his past mistakes as legal evidence to gain the right to destroy him. And what did Jesus do? He didn't just say a prayer in the way we usually think of prayer. The word translated "prayed" in that passage means to make a righteous decree. Jesus stood before the court and He declared Peter righteous, innocent, and forgiven on the basis of what the cross would accomplish. That's legislative prayer. That's a righteous decree issued from a position of authority that shut down the enemy's legal case before it could succeed.

That's what you're called to do on behalf of the people in your *metron*.

When the enemy builds a case against your child, your marriage, your church, you don't just ask God to help. You enter the courtroom. You approach through the blood of Jesus Christ, which is your only standing in that court. Not your years of fasting. Not your track record of ministry. The righteousness of Christ alone is your credential. And from that place, you build a counter-case from the Word of God. You issue a righteous decree that shuts down what the enemy is claiming. You don't beg. You don't plead from a position of weakness. You stand as part of the government of God and you legislate what heaven has already declared.

There's a story that illustrates the difference between principle-based legislative prayer and just asking God to fix something. In Mark 6, Jesus was with a crowd of five thousand men, not counting women and children. It was late. The disciples wanted to send the people away to find food. Jesus said no. He told the disciples to feed them. A boy offered five loaves and two fish. Jesus blessed it, broke it, and gave it to the disciples with a command: go distribute it. Watch what He did there. He didn't just perform a miracle. He activated a principle. He got the disciples to become the conduit of the miracle. He made them participants in the legislative act. And because they activated that altar of righteousness, because they gave and served, when they got on a boat later and a storm came that was meant to kill them, Jesus showed up and saved them. The altar they had built through the act of feeding the multitude created a legal claim on heaven's protection. They could have prayed in that boat. It wouldn't have been enough in that moment. What saved them was the principle they had already activated. That's the difference between knowing how to pray and knowing which principle to activate in the spirit. Legislative prayer isn't just about saying the right words. It's about knowing the right kingdom principle to apply to the situation you're facing.

The altar you build before God is the source of your legislative authority. You are only as strong as the altar you've built through prayer, through fasting, through obedience, through consistent time in the Word. The person who has built a deep altar before God doesn't just pray. They decree. They don't just ask. They legislate. And when they stand before the courts of heaven and issue a decree based on a specific scripture that addresses the situation they're facing, heaven is obligated to enforce it. Not because of who they are. Because of the Word of God they're standing on and the blood of Jesus that gives them legal standing to stand on it.

As a *Shamar* watchman, this shifts everything about how you approach intercession. You're not just a person who prays a lot. You're a legislative representative of the government of God, standing in the gap between heaven and earth, making sure that what God has declared in His Word becomes the legal reality over the territory He's assigned to you. That's the *Shamar* call at its deepest level. Not just guarding the gate. Governing the atmosphere through righteous decrees that the enemy cannot legally override.

The Ecclesia Contract

There's a word that Jesus used that most believers have heard their whole lives without understanding what it actually means. When He said in Matthew 16:18, "On this rock I will build my church," the word translated "church" in the original Greek is *ecclesia.* Not a building. Not a Sunday gathering. Not a religious institution. Ecclesia means the judicial or legislative people of God. In the ancient Greek world, the *ecclesia* was the governing assembly of a city. It was the body of citizens who had the authority to make binding decisions on behalf of the community. They passed laws. They issued decrees. They governed.

That's what Jesus said He was building.

When Jesus said, "On this rock I will build my *ecclesia*, and the gates of hell shall not prevail against it," He wasn't just promising that the church would survive. He was declaring that He was establishing a governmental body on the earth with the authority to legislate in the spirit realm. You are part of that body. Every Spirit-filled believer is. And that means you're not just a member of a religious organization. You're a member of God's government. You hold a governmental position in the kingdom of heaven. And that position comes with legal authority to make binding decisions in the spirit that heaven is obligated to enforce.

Then Jesus said something that makes this even more specific. He said, "I will give you the keys of the kingdom of heaven. Whatever you bind on earth shall be bound in heaven, and whatever you loose on earth shall be loosed in heaven." That word "bind" and that word "loose" are contractual terms. They're legal language. In the ancient world, these words were used to describe the making and breaking of contracts. Whatever you bind, you're putting into a spiritual contract. Whatever you loose, you're releasing from one. When you bind something in prayer, you're making a legally binding spiritual agreement that what you've bound cannot come undone. When you loose something, it cannot be bound. And heaven enforces the contract.

That's not a metaphor. That's a legal reality in the spirit realm.

So when you pray as part of the *ecclesia*, you're not just expressing a desire to God and hoping He agrees. You're functioning as a member of His government, issuing spiritual contracts that carry the weight of heaven's authority behind them. The enemy can't just ignore a binding decree made by a member of the *ecclesia* who is standing in right relationship with God through the blood of Jesus. He has to respond. He has to comply. Because the court has ruled and the books have recorded the decree.

This also means that your approach to prayer needs to shift from a posture of requesting to a posture of legislating. Not that you never bring requests to God. You do. Petition prayer is real and it matters. But when you're operating as a watchman, when you're standing in the gap for your family or your church or your city, you're not coming to God as a beggar hoping He'll do something nice. You're coming as an ambassador who knows the laws of their home country and is applying those laws to the situation in front of them. An ambassador doesn't beg the government they represent. They represent it. They speak on its behalf. They apply its laws with confidence because they know the government is behind them.

That's who you are in prayer. You're an ambassador of heaven, applying the laws of God's kingdom to the territory He's assigned to you.

Think about what it means to approach the courts of heaven as a member of the *ecclesia*. The first thing you need to understand is that you don't enter that courtroom on your own merit. If your adversary, meaning the enemy, has anything on you, the Bible says to make it right before you get to the King. That means you come to the courts of heaven through repentance first. You come through the blood of Jesus Christ. His righteousness is your standing. His merit is your case. Not your years of faithful prayer. Not your track record of intercession. Christ in you is the hope of glory, and Christ's righteousness is the only credential the courtroom of heaven accepts.

Once you're standing in the court through the blood of Jesus, you can begin to build your case. And a case in the courts of heaven is built from the Word of God. You find the scripture that speaks directly to the situation you're bringing before God. You don't come with vague feelings or general concerns. You come with evidence. You come with the Word. "God, your Word says in Isaiah 54:17 that no weapon formed against me shall prosper. I'm standing on that decree right now over my family. The weapon the enemy has formed against my child's mind is null and void according to your Word. I decree it. I bind it. I make it a spiritual contract right now in the name of Jesus." That's legislative prayer. That's the *ecclesia* functioning the way God designed it.

There's also a covenantal dimension to this that watchmen need to understand. God is governmental, but He's also a Father. And as a Father who is also a King, He responds to the covenants and agreements His children make with Him. The Bible shows this pattern repeatedly. For the love of David, God covered Solomon's mistakes. For the covenant made with Abraham, God extended mercy to entire generations. These weren't just sentimental gestures. They were governmental responses to covenantal agreements that had been established in the spirit. When you make a covenant with God, when you say, "God, I'm committing to this specific thing, and I'm asking you to move in this specific way over my family," you're engaging the governmental nature of a Father who is also a King. He responds to covenant. He honors vows. He enforces agreements made through His Word and His name.

Think about a woman named Cecelia, a 42-year-old intercessor who has been praying for her adult son Marcus for seven years. He walked away from God in his early twenties. She's been praying general prayers for him. "God, save Marcus. God, bring him back. God, touch his heart." All sincere. All real. But one day, someone teaches her about legislative prayer and the courts of heaven. And she shifts her approach. She goes before God through the blood of Jesus. She finds a specific scripture, Jeremiah 31:17, "There is hope for your future, says the Lord, and your children shall come back to their own country." She builds her case. She says, "God, your Word is my evidence. I'm standing before your court right now as part of your *ecclesia.* I'm binding every spirit of deception that has been blinding my son's eyes. I'm loosing the spirit of revelation over his mind. I'm making this a binding spiritual contract in the name of Jesus." And then she makes a vow. "God, if you turn my son's heart, I will dedicate the rest of my prayer life to standing in the gap for other prodigal children in my city." That's a covenant. That's a governmental agreement between a member of the *ecclesia* and the King of heaven. And God, who is governmental and who honors covenant, responds to that kind of prayer in a way that's different from the general petitions she'd been making for seven years.

This is the power of understanding the *ecclesia* contract. You're not just a person who prays. You're a member of God's government. You have legal standing in the courts of heaven. You have the authority to bind and loose. You have the ability to make covenants that God honors. And every decree you issue from that place of right standing through the blood of Jesus carries the full weight of heaven's authority behind it. The enemy knows it. The angels know it. And the books of heaven record it.

The *Shamar* anointing over your family and your city isn't just about showing up to pray every day. It's about showing up as a member of the government of God, with a case built from the Word, standing in the right court, through the right blood, issuing the right decrees. That's what it means to carry the *Shamar* call at a legislative level. That's what it means to be the *ecclesia.*

Putting It Into Practice

Legislative prayer isn't complicated. But it does require a different approach than what most people are used to. It requires you to think like a member of a government rather than a person making a request. It requires you to come with evidence, meaning scripture, rather than just feelings. And it requires you to speak your decrees out loud with the confidence of someone who knows they're standing in the right court with the right credentials.

Here's your specific sequence for building and issuing a legislative prayer decree. Follow these steps exactly, at least the first few times, until the pattern becomes natural.

Step one: identify the situation that needs to shift. Be specific. Don't pray in generalities. Name the exact thing you're bringing before the courts of heaven. Is it a pattern of confusion in your household? A spirit of division moving toward your church? A specific attack on your child's identity or their faith? A financial pattern that keeps repeating no matter what you do? Name it clearly. Write it down in one sentence. The more specific you are, the more targeted your decree will be.

Step two: enter the court through the blood of Jesus. Before you say anything else, speak this out loud: "Father, I come before your court right now not on the basis of my own righteousness but through the blood of Jesus Christ. His righteousness is my standing. His merit is my credential. I have no case apart from Him, and I bring nothing of my own merit before this court." That's not a ritual. That's a legal positioning. It's you establishing your standing before you present your case. Don't skip it. The enemy will challenge your right to be in that courtroom, and this is how you answer the challenge.

Step three: find your scripture. This is the evidence in your case. Go to the Word of God and find a specific verse or passage that speaks directly to the situation you named in step one. Not a vague, general verse. A specific one that addresses the specific issue. If you're praying against confusion over a family member, find a verse about the God of peace and clarity. If you're praying against division in your church, find a verse about the unity of the body of Christ. If you're praying for a prodigal child, find a verse about God's promise to your children and their children. Write the verse down. This is your legal evidence. This is what you're standing on.

Step four: write out your formal decree. This is the most important step and the one that separates legislative prayer from regular petition. Take the situation you identified and the scripture you found and write out a formal decree. It should be written in the present tense. It should be specific. It should be based directly on the scripture. Here's an example of what this looks like. If you're standing on Isaiah 54:17 for protection over your family, your written decree might read: "By the authority of God's Word in Isaiah 54:17, I decree right now that no weapon formed against my family shall prosper. Every tongue that rises against us in judgment I condemn by the authority of the blood of Jesus. I bind every assignment of the enemy against my household and I loose the protection, peace, and favor of God over every person under this roof. This decree is a binding spiritual contract in the name of Jesus Christ, and I declare it sealed in the courts of heaven." That's a decree. That's legislative prayer in written form.

Step five: speak it out loud. Don't just write it and leave it on paper. Speak it. Romans 10:10 says that with the mouth, confession is made. There's a reason God designed the spoken word as part of how spiritual authority is exercised. When you speak your decree out loud, you're not just expressing a thought. You're issuing a legal statement in the spirit. You're activating the contractual language that Jesus described when He said whatever you bind on earth is bound in heaven. Say it with confidence. Not with arrogance. With the confidence of someone who knows they're standing in the right court with the right credentials and the right evidence.

Step six: hold the decree. Don't speak it once and then go back to worrying. A decree that's been issued needs to be maintained. Come back to it daily. Speak it again. Remind yourself and the spirit realm of what has been legally established. Nehemiah didn't build the wall in a day. He built it gate by gate, day by day, while fighting opposition the entire time. Your legislative prayer is the same. You issue the decree. You hold the line. You keep the decree active through consistent, faith-filled repetition until you see the manifestation of what you've decreed in the natural world.

This week, take one situation from your life or from the life of someone in your *metron* that needs to shift. One specific situation. Walk through all six steps. Write out your formal decree based on a specific scripture. Speak it out loud every day for seven days. Keep a journal of what you observe shifting in the natural during those seven days. You don't need to manufacture evidence. Just watch. And write down what you see. Because when a member of the *ecclesia* stands in the courts of heaven and issues a righteous decree through the blood of Jesus, things move. Not always immediately in the way you expect. But they move. Heaven enforces the contract. The books record the decree. And the *Shamar* anointing over your family and your city grows stronger with every legislative prayer you pray from your post on the wall.

Activation & Reflection

---

1. What is the difference between legislative prayer (establishing God's decrees) and warfare prayer (enforcing them)? How do you currently practice both?

____
____
____
____

2. In which type of prayer — legislative or warfare — do you feel most confident? Which needs to be developed in you?

____
____
____
____

3. What spiritual decrees has God given you to establish over your territory? Have you been consistently declaring them?

____
____
____
____

4. How does understanding the Ecclesia — the governing assembly of believers — change your view of the local church's role in intercession?

____

____

____

____

5. Describe a specific battle in your life or community that calls for legislative prayer rather than reactive warfare. How will you approach it?

____

____

____

____

A Legislative Prayer

Father, I come before Your heavenly council not just as a petitioner but as a kingdom legislator. I take my seat in heavenly places in Christ Jesus. I declare that what You have written in Your Word stands as eternal law over my life and territory. I enforce the decrees of heaven. I bind what You have bound, and I loose what You have loosed. Let Your kingdom come and Your will be done on earth as it is in heaven. In Jesus' name, Amen.

CHAPTER 8

Building Your Case in the Courts of Heaven

There's a moment in every serious prayer life where something shifts. You stop begging and you start building. You stop hoping God notices and you start presenting your case with the confidence of someone who knows the law is on their side. That shift doesn't happen by accident. It happens when you finally understand that God isn't just a loving Father. He's also a Judge. And judges don't respond to emotion alone. They respond to evidence. They respond to legal arguments. They respond to cases that are built on the right foundation and presented with the right authority.

That's what this chapter is about.

You've already learned about the courts of heaven. You've seen how legislative prayer works. You understand the *ecclesia* contract and what it means to bind and loose with legal authority. Now it's time to get specific. Not just the concept of presenting your case, but the actual mechanics of how you do it. What evidence do you bring? What principles do you activate? How do you remind God of promises He made over your life without it sounding like you're trying to manipulate Him? These aren't small questions. And the answers will change the way you pray for the rest of your life.

Presenting the Evidence

When a lawyer walks into a courtroom, they don't walk in empty-handed. They walk in with a file. Evidence. Documents. Precedent. They've done the research. They know the law. They know what their client is owed and they know how to argue for it based on what's already been established. That's the posture you need to carry into the courts of heaven. Not timid. Not uncertain. Not whispering your requests and hoping for the best. You walk in with your file. You walk in with the Word of God in your hand and the blood of Jesus as your credential, and you build your case.

God is governmental. He never stops being a Father, but He's also always a King. And kings operate through order, through covenant, through the legal structures they've established. When Moses stood before God after Israel had sinned with the golden calf, God told Moses He was going to destroy the entire nation. Moses didn't just cry and hope God changed His mind. He built a case. He said, "Remember Abraham, Isaac, and Israel, your servants, to whom you swore by your own self." He reminded God of the covenant. He brought the promise back before the Judge. And the Bible says God relented from the disaster He had planned. That wasn't Moses manipulating God. That was Moses understanding how the courts of heaven work. He found the legal ground, the covenant God had already established, and he stood on it.

That's exactly what you're called to do.

The Word of God is your primary evidence in the courts of heaven. Every promise in Scripture is a legal document. Every covenant God established is a binding agreement that He will not violate. When you bring His Word back to Him in prayer, you're not reminding Him of something He forgot. He doesn't forget. You're activating the legal standing of His promise over your specific situation. You're saying, "God, you said this. I'm standing on it. I'm bringing it before your court as the basis of my petition." That's not arrogance. That's faith operating in its most precise form.

Think about how Jesus stood at the tomb of Lazarus. He didn't say, "Father, if it be your will, could you maybe consider raising Lazarus?" He said, "Father, I thank you that you have heard me. I know that you always hear me." That's the confidence of someone who knows they have legal standing before the Judge. He wasn't uncertain. He wasn't hoping. He was operating from a place of settled authority, and He issued a command that death itself had to obey. James 5:16 says the effective prayer of a righteous person accomplishes much. The word "effective" is the key. Effective prayer is aimed prayer. It's prayer built on a specific legal foundation. It knows what it's asking for and why it has the right to ask for it.

There's a difference between effective prayers and ineffective ones, and that difference isn't about how loud you pray or how long you pray. It's about whether you're praying from a place of legal standing. When you come before God timid and uncertain, treating your prayers like a lottery ticket you're hoping will win, God counts that as double-mindedness. James 1:6-7 says the double-minded person shouldn't think they'll receive anything from the Lord. But when you come as a son or daughter, when you come with the boldness of someone who knows their Father and knows His Word, the atmosphere changes entirely. Think about a child who knows their parent well. They don't tiptoe around the house hoping their parent will be in a good mood. They walk in with confidence because they know they're loved and they know what they're asking for is reasonable. That's the posture of someone presenting evidence in the courts of heaven. Not demanding. Not manipulating. Confident. Because you know the law is on your side.

Now here's the part that most believers miss. Presenting evidence in the courts of heaven isn't just about quoting scripture. It's also about presenting the evidence of your faithfulness. Your history with God matters in that courtroom. The covenants you've made and kept, the vows you've fulfilled, the acts of obedience you've walked out even when it cost you something, these things create a legal record in the spirit. God said to Solomon, "Because you have done this, and have not kept my covenant and my statutes, I will tear the kingdom from you." But He also said, "Nevertheless I will not do it in your days, for the sake of your father David." David's faithfulness created a legal covering that extended to his son. Your acts of kingdom obedience build a legal record that the courts of heaven recognize. That record becomes part of your case.

When you make a covenant with God, when you say, "God, I'm committing to this specific act of obedience, and I'm asking you to respond in this specific way," you're engaging the governmental nature of a King who honors His word. He responds to covenant. He enforces agreements. The Bible calls these vows, and they're not just spiritual feelings. They're legal agreements that carry weight in the courts of heaven. Abraham made covenants. David made covenants. And God's response to both of them went beyond what their natural circumstances deserved, because the covenant created a legal claim that God honored even when the person fell short.

You have that same access right now.

Think about a man named Daniel, a 38-year-old who has been interceding for his prodigal son for four years. He's been praying general prayers. "God, save my son. God, bring him back." Sincere prayers. Real prayers. But one day someone teaches him about presenting evidence in the courts of heaven. He goes before God differently. He comes through the blood of Jesus first. He finds a specific scripture,

Acts 16:31, "Believe in the Lord Jesus and you will be saved, you and your household." He presents it as evidence. He says, "God, your Word established a household covenant. My son belongs to this household. I'm standing on this promise as my legal ground." Then he presents the evidence of his own faithfulness. He says, "God, I have served you for twenty-two years. I've kept my vows. I've stayed in my post. I'm presenting my history with you as part of this case, not as my righteousness, but as evidence of the covenant we've built together." And then he makes a decree. He doesn't beg. He legislates. He says, "On the basis of your Word and the blood of Jesus, I bind every spirit of deception over my son's mind and I loose the spirit of revelation and conviction over him right now." That's a case. That's evidence-based, covenant-grounded, blood-bought legislative prayer. And it carries a completely different weight than four years of hopeful wishing.

Here's your specific practice for presenting evidence in the courts of heaven. Take the situation you're currently interceding for and do this in writing before you pray it out loud. Write the name of the person or situation at the top of a blank page. Directly below that, write the specific scripture that addresses this situation. Not a general verse. A verse that speaks directly to what you're asking for. Below that, write one sentence describing a specific act of faithfulness or covenant you've made with God that's relevant to this request. Something you've done, something you've kept, something you've walked out in obedience. Then write your decree in present tense based on both the scripture and the covenant. Speak it out loud over that person or situation. That written structure is your file. That's what you carry into the courtroom. Do this for every major intercession you're carrying right now. It will take time. It requires thought. But it will transform your prayer from general petition into targeted legislative intercession that the courts of heaven recognize and respond to.

One more thing about presenting evidence. You come into that courtroom through the blood of Jesus alone. Not your track record. Not your years of fasting. Not your position in ministry. The blood of Jesus is your credential. His righteousness is your standing. And when you enter through that blood, you're entering as a son or daughter of the King, with full legal access to everything His kingdom provides. That's not a small thing. That's the most powerful legal standing in the universe. Use it.

Activating the Principle of Psalm 41

There are times when prayer alone isn't the right tool for the moment. Not because prayer is weak, but because the situation calls for a specific kingdom principle to be activated, not just a petition to be offered. This is one of the most important distinctions a watchman can learn. God designed the kingdom to operate through specific principles, and those principles carry legal weight in the courts of heaven when they're activated through obedience. The person who knows which principle to activate at the right moment doesn't just pray. They legislate through action.

Psalm 41:1-3 says this: "Blessed is he who considers the poor. The Lord will deliver him in time of trouble. The Lord will preserve him and keep him alive, and he will be blessed on the earth. You will not deliver him to the will of his enemies. The Lord will strengthen him on his bed of illness." Read that carefully. It's a covenant promise. It's a legal agreement built into the fabric of the kingdom. The person who considers the poor, who actively gives to and serves those in need, builds a legal hedge around themselves. They create a record in the courts of heaven that says: this person has activated the principle of generosity and compassion. And when trouble comes, when the enemy tries to move against them, that record becomes a legal defense.

Jesus understood this principle and He used it strategically.

In Mark 6, when five thousand men plus women and children were gathered and it was late in the day, Jesus didn't just perform a miracle for the crowd. He activated a principle. He told His disciples to feed the people. He could have handed out the food Himself. But He deliberately put the disciples in the position of being the givers. He made them the ones who served the multitude. He made them the ones who activated the altar of generosity. Why? Because He could see what was coming. He knew they were about to get on a boat and face a storm that was designed to kill them.

And He knew that the prayer they could pray in that boat wouldn't be enough to save them in that specific moment. What would save them was the legal hedge they were about to build by feeding the multitude. So He set it up. He activated the principle before the crisis arrived. And when the storm came and the boat was being tossed and the disciples thought they were going to die, Jesus showed up and saved them. Not because of their faith in that moment. Because of the altar they had built through their act of obedience just hours before.

That's what it means to pre-pray through kingdom principles. You don't wait for the crisis to show up and then scramble to find a scripture. You build the altar before the storm. You activate the principles of the kingdom in your daily life so that when trouble comes, there's already a legal record in the courts of heaven that the enemy has to contend with. The hedge is already up. The protection has already been established. The case has already been built. And when the enemy tries to move against you, he runs into a legal wall that your obedience constructed before he ever showed up.

This principle extends beyond generosity. Every act of kingdom obedience builds a legal record. When you forgive someone who wronged you, you're activating the principle of Matthew 6:14 and building a legal claim on God's forgiveness in your own life. When you honor your spiritual covering, you're activating the principle of Hebrews 13:17 and building a legal hedge of protection over your own assignment. When you tithe faithfully, you're activating the principle of Malachi 3:10 and building a legal defense against the devourer over your finances. Every principle you activate through obedience becomes a file in your case. Every act of faithfulness adds evidence to your record in the courts of heaven.

The enemy knows this. That's why he works so hard to get believers to compromise in these areas. He's not just trying to get you to sin. He's trying to empty your file. He's trying to remove the evidence from your case. Because a watchman with an empty file has no legal ground to stand on when he brings a case before the courts of heaven. But a watchman who has been consistently activating kingdom principles through obedience walks into that courtroom with a full file. And the enemy has no counter-argument for a life lived in covenant faithfulness.

Here's the specific practice for activating the principle of Psalm 41 in your life right now. Identify one act of generosity or compassion that you can do this week that's connected to the specific intercession you're carrying. If you're praying for someone in financial need, give to them specifically. If you're interceding for the poor in your city, do something concrete this week to serve them. If you're standing in the gap for someone who's sick, visit them, bring them food, sit with them. The act doesn't have to be large. It has to be intentional. It has to be a deliberate activation of the Psalm 41 principle over the specific situation you're praying about. When you do it, do it consciously. Say out loud before you act: "Father, I'm activating the principle of

Psalm 41 right now. I'm building a legal hedge through this act of kingdom obedience. I'm presenting this before your court as evidence in my case for the breakthrough I'm believing for over this situation." Then do the act. That's not a formula. That's a watchman who understands how the kingdom works and uses that understanding to build their case before trouble arrives.

The disciples didn't know they were building their own lifeline when they handed out those loaves and fish. But Jesus knew. And He set it up on purpose. As a *Shamar* watchman, you don't have to wait for Jesus to set it up for you. You can set it up yourself. You can look at the people in your *metron*, see what's coming against them in the spirit, and begin to activate kingdom principles on their behalf right now. You can build their hedge before the storm arrives. That's what it means to stand in the gap. Not just praying after the breach. Building the wall before the breach happens.

Reminding God of Your Purpose

There's a specific kind of prayer that carries unusual power. It's the prayer of a person who stands before God and says, "I haven't finished yet." It's the prayer that points to an unfulfilled destiny, an unfinished assignment, a promise that was spoken over your life that hasn't come to pass yet. And it's one of the most powerful legal arguments a watchman can bring before the courts of heaven.

Purpose is what keeps you alive. That's not a metaphor. It's a spiritual reality. When God writes a book about your life before you're born, when He records every day that's been ordained for you before one of them comes to be, that book contains an assignment. A specific reason for your existence. A specific work that only you can do in the specific time and place God positioned you in. And as long as that assignment is unfinished, you have legal grounds to stand before God and say, "I'm not done yet."

There's a story in 2 Kings 4 that captures this perfectly. A Shunammite woman had received a prophetic promise that she would have a son. The son was born. He grew. And then one day, the boy died suddenly. She didn't collapse in despair. She didn't accept it as final. She went straight to the man of God, and when she found him, she asked one piercing question: "Did I ask you for a son? Did I say, give me a son?" She was building a case. She was reminding the prophet of the promise that had been spoken. She was saying, "This prophecy came from God. It hasn't been fulfilled in full. A son who dies in childhood is not the complete fulfillment of what was promised." And because she refused to accept a conclusion that contradicted the promise, because she brought the unfinished prophecy back before the courts of heaven through her declaration, the boy was raised from the dead. Resurrection power came from the reminder of destiny.

That's the principle of reminding God of your purpose. You're not telling God something He doesn't know. He wrote the book. He knows every word in it. But when you stand before Him and say, "The assignment you wrote over my life isn't finished yet. The prophecy you spoke over me hasn't been fulfilled yet. The destiny you placed in my heart before I was born is still waiting," you're activating a legal argument that carries tremendous weight in the courts of heaven. You're giving God a reason, not that He needs one, but in the legal framework of the courts, you're presenting a case for why the outcome needs to shift.

Psalm 139 is your foundational text for this kind of prayer. Verse 16 says, "Your eyes saw my unformed substance. In your book were written, every one of them, the days that were formed for me, when as yet there was none of them." That book is your legal document. Every day God ordained for you is recorded in it. Every assignment. Every destiny moment. Every person you were designed to reach. Every prayer you were created to pray. It's all in the book. And when the enemy tries to cut you off prematurely, when circumstances or attacks try to bring your story to an end before the book is finished, you have legal grounds to stand before the Judge and say, "There are still pages in my book that haven't been lived yet. My assignment isn't complete. My destiny isn't fulfilled. I'm presenting the unfinished chapters of my book as evidence before this court."

This is also the prayer that shifts life-and-death situations. Hezekiah in Isaiah 38 is one of the clearest examples. God sent the prophet Isaiah to tell him that he was going to die. His time was up. The decree had been issued.

Hezekiah turned his face to the wall and prayed. He reminded God of his faithfulness. He said, "Remember, Lord, how I have walked before you faithfully and with wholehearted devotion and have done what is good in your eyes." And God, before Isaiah had even left the middle court, sent him back to Hezekiah with a new word. Fifteen more years. The decree was reversed. Not because Hezekiah argued louder than the first decree. But because he built a case. He reminded God of his faithfulness and his unfinished assignment. And the courts of heaven responded.

Your unfinished assignment is one of the most powerful pieces of evidence you can bring before the courts of heaven. Not in a prideful way. Not as if God owes you something because of your greatness. But in the humble, faith-filled awareness that God doesn't waste assignments. He doesn't call people to destinies He never intended to fulfill. He doesn't place burning desires in your heart just to let them die unfulfilled. When you stand before Him and say, "God, you wrote this over my life. You placed this desire in me. You spoke this promise. It isn't finished yet," you're standing on the faithfulness of God Himself. You're appealing to His own character. And that's an argument He never dismisses.

The Water Gate in the Nehemiah roadmap represents this principle. It's the gate of rebirthing purpose. After the valley, after the Dung Gate, after the fresh filling of the Fountain Gate, God brings you back to the original assignment. He says, "Remember what I told you? I haven't forgotten it. The valley didn't cancel it. It prepared you to carry it." The Water Gate is where God reminds you of your purpose. But you can also bring your purpose back to Him. You can stand before Him and say, "I'm reminding you of what you wrote about me. I'm presenting the unfinished chapters of my book as my case. I'm not done yet."

As a *Shamar* watchman, this principle applies not just to your own life but to the lives of the people in your *metron*. When you're interceding for someone whose destiny seems to be stuck or threatened, one of the most powerful prayers you can pray is this: "God, this person has an unfinished assignment. You wrote a book about them before they were born. The pages of their destiny haven't all been lived yet. I'm standing before your court and I'm presenting their unfinished purpose as evidence that the enemy's plan to cut them off short cannot succeed. Their story isn't over. Their assignment isn't complete. I bind every premature conclusion the enemy is trying to write over their life, and I decree that every page God ordained for them will be lived in full, in the name of Jesus."

That's not a small prayer. That's a watchman standing in the gap between someone's present circumstances and their God-ordained destiny, using the legal principle of unfinished purpose as evidence before the courts of heaven. That's the *Shamar* anointing functioning at its deepest level.

Think about a hypothetical scenario. Consider a woman named Miriam, a 51-year-old who has been in full-time ministry for fifteen years. She's been going through a season of serious illness that has kept her from her assignment for eight months. She's been praying for healing, but the prayers feel like they're hitting a ceiling. Then someone teaches her about reminding God of her purpose. She goes before the courts of heaven through the blood of Jesus. She opens Psalm 139 and she reads verse 16 out loud. She says, "God, you wrote a book about me. I'm only halfway through the chapters you ordained for me. The nations I haven't yet reached, the people I haven't yet prayed for, the assignment you placed in my heart twenty years ago that's only been partially fulfilled, I'm presenting all of it before your court right now as evidence. My story isn't finished. My book isn't closed. I bind every premature end the enemy is trying to assign to my life, and I decree that I will live and not die and declare the works of the Lord, according to Psalm 118:17." That prayer isn't wishful thinking. It's a legal decree built on the principle of unfinished destiny. And it carries a weight that a general prayer for healing doesn't carry, because it's built on the specific legal ground of an unfinished assignment recorded in the books of heaven.

Here's the specific practice for praying this kind of prayer over your own life. Set aside thirty minutes this week for what you could call a destiny review. Open your Bible to Psalm 139 and read it slowly out loud. Then get a journal and write down every significant promise, prophecy, or God-given desire that's been placed in your heart that hasn't been fully fulfilled yet. Not the things you want. The things God specifically put in you. The desires that have been consistent across years and seasons. The prophetic words that were spoken over you that haven't come to pass yet. The assignments you know God gave you that are still waiting. Write them all down. That list is your file. That's your evidence of unfinished destiny. Then bring it before the courts of heaven. Present each item specifically. Say out loud, "God, this is still in my book. This hasn't been fulfilled yet. I'm presenting it before your court as evidence that my assignment isn't complete and that every attack of the enemy designed to cut me off short has no legal ground to stand on." Do this once. Then do it again the next time the enemy tries to convince you that your story is over or your best days are behind you. Because the book God wrote about you doesn't end until every page He ordained has been lived. And you're the watchman who knows how to stand on that truth in the courts of heaven.

Your Case, Your Post, Your Breakthrough

Everything in this chapter has been moving toward one practical reality. You can build a case before the courts of heaven that produces real, specific, legally binding results in the spirit realm. Not through luck. Not through the right emotional state. Through the right evidence, the right principles, and the right legal standing through the blood of Jesus Christ.

Building a case is the work of a watchman who has taken their post seriously. It's the natural outgrowth of everything you've been learning. You know your *metron.* You're under covering. You understand legislative prayer. And now you know how to walk into the courts of heaven with a file, with evidence, with covenant ground, with activated kingdom principles, and with the unfinished pages of your God-ordained destiny as your legal argument.

The recap is simple. Presenting evidence means bringing the specific Word of God and the record of your covenant faithfulness before the Judge as the legal basis for your petition. Activating the principle of Psalm 41 means building your legal hedge before the storm arrives by consistently walking in kingdom obedience, especially generosity and compassion toward those in need. Reminding God of your purpose means standing before the courts of heaven with the unfinished chapters of your book and declaring that the enemy's plans to cut you off short have no legal ground.

Together, these three practices form the foundation of what it means to build a case in the courts of heaven. They're not separate strategies. They work together. Your scripture is the law. Your covenant faithfulness is the precedent. Your unfinished destiny is the argument. And the blood of Jesus is the credential that gives you the right to present all of it before the Judge.

Now here are your action steps. There are three of them. Do all three this week, in order.

The first action step is to find your promise in Psalm 139. Open that chapter and read it slowly. Ask the Holy Spirit to highlight a specific verse that speaks to the destiny God wrote over your life. When a verse lands in your spirit, write it down. That verse is the foundation of your case. It's the legal document you're going to stand on. Below that verse, write in one sentence the specific unfulfilled promise or unfinished assignment in your life that this verse speaks to. Be specific. Not vague. One sentence. That's your case statement. That's what you're bringing before the courts of heaven.

The second action step is to activate one kingdom principle this week that's connected to what you're believing for. Not a random act of generosity. A deliberate, intentional activation of a specific principle that speaks to your specific intercession. If you're standing for healing, serve someone who is sick this week. If you're standing for a financial breakthrough, give to someone in financial need. If you're interceding for a prodigal, fast one meal and consecrate that fast specifically to that person's return. Do it consciously. Declare before God that you're activating this principle as part of your case. Write down what you did and the date you did it. That's evidence in your file.

The third action step is to write out and speak your full legislative decree based on everything in your file. Take your Psalm 139 promise, your covenant faithfulness record, and your activated kingdom principle, and write a formal decree that incorporates all three. It should be no longer than one paragraph. It should be specific, present-tense, and based directly on scripture. Speak it out loud every morning for the next seven days. Not as a ritual. As a legal declaration before the courts of heaven. Each time you speak it, you're reinforcing the legal standing of your case. You're reminding the spirit realm of what has been established. And you're holding the line until the manifestation appears in the natural.

The *Shamar* anointing over your family and your city isn't built on good intentions. It's built on cases that have been carefully constructed, legally grounded, and consistently maintained before the courts of heaven. You're not just a person who prays. You're a guardian who knows the law, knows their rights, and knows how to stand in the gap with the full authority of heaven behind them. That's the watchman God is raising up in this hour. That's who you are. And the case you build in the courts of heaven today is the wall that protects the people you love tomorrow.

Activation & Reflection

---

1. What specific cases do you need to present before the Courts of Heaven right now — for yourself, your family, or your territory?

____

____

____

____

2. What evidence from God's Word will you bring before the heavenly courts to support your petition?

____

____

____

____

3. Have you identified any legal grounds the enemy may be using against you? What must be repented of and revoked?

____

____

____

____

4. How does approaching God as a righteous Judge — rather than only as Father — deepen and expand your prayer life?

____
____
____
____

5. Write a brief 'legal brief' for one situation you are currently interceding over: state the promise, the evidence, and your petition.

____
____
____
____

A Prayer in the Courts of Heaven

Righteous Judge and loving Father, I approach Your heavenly court with confidence through the blood of Jesus. I present Your Word as evidence — Your covenant, Your promises, and Your faithfulness. I cancel every accusation the enemy has brought before You against my life, my family, and my assignment. Let the verdict of heaven be released into the earth. I receive Your ruling with faith and thanksgiving. In Jesus' name, Amen.

CHAPTER 9

The Three Spirits on the Wall

The moment you say yes to standing on the wall, something shifts in the spirit realm. It's not your imagination. It's not coincidence. The enemy knows exactly what you've just committed to, and he responds with a strategy that's older than you are. He doesn't come with something new. He comes with the same three spirits he sent against Nehemiah thousands of years ago when a man of God dared to rebuild what had been broken. And those three spirits are still working today with the same goal they've always had: get you off the wall.

Nehemiah was a builder. He had a God-given assignment to rebuild the walls of Jerusalem, walls that had been broken down and left in ruin. He didn't come with an army. He came with a burden and a blueprint. And the moment he started building, opposition showed up. Not random opposition. Targeted, strategic, multi-pronged opposition designed to pull him away from his post before the wall could be completed. Three specific forces came at him. Sanballat. Tobiah. And the Ashdodites. Three spirits. Three distinct tactics. One goal.

You need to know all three by name.

Because the *Shamar* anointing you carry over your family and your city makes you a target. A watchman who doesn't know what's coming at them is a watchman who can be surprised off the wall. But a watchman who can name the spirit, identify the tactic, and respond with the right weapon stays in their place. They keep building. They keep praying. They keep standing in the gap no matter what comes against them. That's what this chapter is about.

Sanballat: The Spirit of Discouragement

Sanballat was the first one to show up in Nehemiah's story. He didn't come with a sword. He came with words. Specifically, he came with questions designed to make Nehemiah doubt the value of what he was doing. He said things like, "What are these feeble Jews doing? Will they restore things? Will they offer sacrifices? Will they finish in a day? Will they revive the stones out of the heaps of rubbish?" Every question was a seed of discouragement planted in the soil of Nehemiah's assignment. And that's exactly how this spirit operates today.

The spirit of Sanballat doesn't attack your body. It attacks your motivation. It goes after the inner conviction that makes you keep showing up to the wall when nothing visible is happening. It whispers the same things it whispered to Nehemiah. "Look how long you've been praying. You're not seeing anything. Why are you still doing this? What's the point?" If you've been in intercession for any serious length of time, you know that voice. You've heard it. Maybe you've believed it for a season.

That voice is a lie. But it's a very convincing one.

The reason Sanballat is so effective is that he doesn't make things up entirely. He takes a real feeling, the tiredness that comes from consistent intercession, the silence of a season where you can't see results, the weight of praying for the same person year after year without visible change, and he uses that real feeling to build a false conclusion. He takes "I'm tired" and turns it into "this is pointless." He takes "I haven't seen results yet" and turns it into "I never will." He takes the gap between where you are and where you're believing for and fills it with the suggestion that the gap will never close.

Understanding this is everything. Discouragement isn't a personal failure. It's a spiritual attack. It's a tactical move by an enemy who knows that a discouraged watchman is an ineffective one. When you're discouraged, you pray less. You show up less. You believe less. And a watchman who's been pulled back from the wall through discouragement is exactly what the enemy needs to advance his plans in your sphere without resistance.

Think about a hypothetical scenario. Consider a woman named Adrienne, a 37-year-old intercessor who has been standing in the gap for her marriage for three years. She wakes up early. She prays. She fasts. She decrees. But from the outside, things look the same or worse. The tension hasn't lifted. Her husband hasn't changed. And after three years of faithful, consistent intercession, the voice of Sanballat starts getting louder. "Nothing is moving. You're wasting your time. Maybe this marriage is just over." That voice isn't coming from God. It isn't coming from wisdom. It's coming from a spirit whose entire assignment is to make Adrienne step away from her post before the breakthrough arrives. Because Sanballat always shows up loudest right before the wall goes up. That's not a coincidence. It's strategy.

The enemy intensifies discouragement in the seasons closest to breakthrough because he knows the wall is almost complete. He knows that if he can get you off the wall in the final stretch, he wins. So when the voice of Sanballat gets louder, don't interpret it as a sign that nothing is happening. Interpret it as a sign that something is about to happen. The pressure increases before the breakthrough, not after it.

Now here's how you fight this spirit specifically. You don't fight discouragement with more effort. You fight it with truth spoken out loud. Nehemiah's response to Sanballat wasn't to argue or to explain himself. He prayed and he kept building. He didn't come down off the wall to have a conversation with his discourager. He stayed at his post. That's the model. But you also need a specific weapon to silence the voice of "why bother," and that weapon is a warfare decree built directly on the Word of God.

When the spirit of Sanballat comes at you with discouragement about your assignment, speak this decree out loud: "I decree that my labor in the Lord is not in vain, according to 1 Corinthians 15:58. I refuse the spirit of discouragement in the name of Jesus. My assignment is not measured by what I can see right now. It is established by what God declared before I was born. I am still on the wall. I am still building. I will not come down." Say it out loud. Not in your head. Out loud. The spoken decree is what pushes the spirit of Sanballat back. It's what keeps your feet planted on the wall when everything in you wants to walk away.

There's also a practical discipline that guards you against Sanballat's long-term strategy. Keep a record of what God has already done in your sphere. Write down every answered prayer, every shift you've seen, every moment where something moved that you know was the result of your intercession. When the voice of discouragement comes and says you're not seeing anything, open that record. Read it out loud. Remind yourself and the spirit realm of what has already been established through your prayers. A watchman who keeps a record of God's faithfulness has a weapon that Sanballat cannot touch. Because you can't argue with a documented history of breakthrough.

The spirit of Sanballat wants you to measure your effectiveness by what you can see right now. But the *Shamar* watchman measures effectiveness by faithfulness to the post. You weren't called to produce visible results on a schedule you control. You were called to stand in the gap and keep building until God says the wall is complete. Stay on the wall.

Tobiah: The Spirit of Slander

After Sanballat came Tobiah. And if Sanballat's attack was internal, aimed at your motivation, Tobiah's attack is external, aimed at your reputation. Tobiah was a mocker. He didn't just question the work. He mocked the worker. In Nehemiah 4:3, he said, "Even what they are building, if a fox goes up on it he will break down their stone wall." He was saying that everything Nehemiah was building was so weak, so worthless, that even a small animal could knock it over. He was attacking not just the project but the person behind it. And that's exactly what the spirit of Tobiah does to watchmen today.

The spirit of slander comes to discredit you. Its goal isn't just to hurt your feelings. Its goal is much more specific and much more dangerous. It wants to make the people in your sphere unable to receive from the anointing you carry. Think about that. If the enemy can get the people you're assigned to guard to doubt who you are, to question your character, to write you off as untrustworthy, then your intercession for them loses its relational weight. The people who need what you carry stop being able to receive it. And the enemy wins without ever having to confront the anointing directly. He just discredits the vessel that carries it.

This is why the spirit of Tobiah always attacks character. Not just behavior. Character. It spreads stories. It highlights past mistakes. It takes things out of context. It puts a narrative around you that paints you as unqualified, untrustworthy, or hypocritical. And it does this most aggressively right when God is about to use you in a significant way. Because if it can get people to dismiss you before they receive from you, the anointing you carry never reaches them.

The most important thing to understand about Tobiah's tactic is this: his goal is never just to hurt you. His goal is to cut off the people in your sphere from what God placed in you for them. When someone slanders a watchman, they're not just attacking a person. They're attacking the spiritual supply line that person represents to everyone in their *metron*. The enemy knows that if he can get people to reject the vessel, they reject the anointing. And a rejected anointing can't guard anyone.

Nehemiah's response to Tobiah is one of the most instructive things in the entire book. He didn't stop building to defend himself. He didn't write a letter explaining his character. He didn't gather people together to set the record straight. He prayed. He said, "Hear, O our God, how we are despised." He brought the attack to God and then he kept building. He refused to let Tobiah's mockery pull him off the wall and into a public defense of himself. Because he understood something that every watchman needs to understand: the moment you come off the wall to defend your reputation, you've already lost the battle. You've handed the enemy exactly what he wanted. You've stopped building and started performing for an audience that was never supposed to be your judge.

God is your judge. His opinion of you is the only one that carries legal weight in the spirit. What Tobiah says about you has no authority in heaven. The courts of heaven don't evaluate you based on the slander of your enemy. They evaluate you based on the record of your faithfulness and the righteousness of Christ that covers you. When you know that, slander loses its power to pull you off the wall.

But you do need a specific response to the spirit of Tobiah when it comes. Here's what that looks like in practice. When you become aware that slander is being spread about you, do three things in this order. First, pray specifically against the spirit behind it. Don't pray against the person. Pray against the spirit of slander and defamation that's using them. Say out loud: "I bind the spirit of Tobiah that's operating against my calling and my character right now in the name of Jesus. I decree that every lie spoken against me falls to the ground and bears no fruit. I decree that the people God has assigned to receive from my anointing are protected from this deception and that their ears remain open to what God placed in me for them." That's a targeted decree against the specific goal of the spirit, which is to cut off your sphere from what you carry.

Second, refuse to make defending yourself your primary occupation. You can address a specific lie if wisdom requires it. But don't let it become your focus. Don't let Tobiah's narrative become the thing you're most known for talking about. Stay focused on the assignment. Keep building. The wall going up is a better defense of your character than anything you can say in your own defense.

Third, keep your identity anchored in what God says about you. Not what feels true in the moment of the attack. What God declared over you before you were born. Read Psalm 139 out loud over yourself when the spirit of slander is loud. Read Isaiah 54:17 out loud: "No weapon formed against you shall prosper, and every tongue that rises against you in judgment you shall condemn." That's not wishful thinking. That's a legal decree from the courts of heaven about what slander is allowed to accomplish in your life. It cannot prosper. Not because you're perfect. Because the blood of Jesus covers you and the assignment God gave you is sealed in heaven's books.

The spirit of Tobiah is most dangerous when you let it make you more concerned with your reputation than with your assignment. A watchman who spends all their energy managing what people think of them has no energy left to guard the gate. Stay focused on what God called you to do. Let Him manage your reputation. He's better at it than you are.

The Ashdodite: The Spirit of Confusion

The third spirit is the most subtle of the three. Sanballat attacks your motivation. Tobiah attacks your reputation. But the Ashdodite spirit attacks something even more fundamental. It attacks your mind. Specifically, it attacks your ability to think clearly about your calling, your identity, and your assignment. It brings a fog into your thinking so thick that you can no longer hold onto what God told you. You start doubting what was once clear. You second-guess what God specifically said. You feel disconnected from the certainty that used to anchor your prayer life. That's the Ashdodite spirit at work.

In Nehemiah 4:7-8, the Ashdodites joined with Sanballat and Tobiah and conspired together to fight against Jerusalem and to cause confusion. That word is important. Confusion. Not just opposition. Not just warfare. Confusion. The goal wasn't to defeat Nehemiah through force. It was to cloud his thinking so badly that he couldn't function effectively in his assignment. A confused watchman can't hear clearly from heaven. A confused intercessor can't pray with precision. A confused guardian can't identify what's coming through the gate because everything looks the same through the fog.

This spirit attacks what could be called the mind gate. In the same way that Jerusalem had physical gates that controlled what came in and out of the city, your mind has a gate. Your ability to think clearly, to hear from God accurately, to hold onto the truth of your calling, all of that flows through the mind gate. And the Ashdodite spirit's entire assignment is to compromise that gate. To flood it with so much noise, doubt, and mental fog that you can no longer distinguish God's voice from the enemy's. You can no longer hold a clear picture of what God told you to do. You feel spiritually scattered, unable to focus, unable to pray with any sense of direction.

One of the most recognizable signs that the Ashdodite spirit is operating against you is when you suddenly can't remember why you're doing what you're doing. You've been a watchman. You've been standing in the gap. And then one day you wake up and it all feels distant and uncertain. The clarity you had is gone. The conviction that used to fuel your intercession feels hollow. You're not in sin. You haven't walked away from God. But something has clouded your ability to see your assignment clearly. That's not a spiritual crisis. That's a spiritual attack. And it requires a specific response.

The Ashdodite spirit also works through information overload. It floods your mind with so many voices, so many opinions, so many conflicting things, that you can't hear the one voice that matters. In the age we're living in, this spirit has more tools than ever. Social media. News cycles. Constant noise. A watchman who doesn't guard their mind gate against this flood of information will find their spiritual clarity eroding slowly, almost imperceptibly, until one day they realize they haven't heard from God clearly in weeks.

Not because God stopped speaking. Because the noise got too loud.

Here's how you recognize this spirit operating against you in a specific way. You'll notice three things happening at the same time. First, your prayer life starts feeling mechanical and dry even though you haven't changed your habits. Second, you start questioning specific things God told you in the past, things that were clear and settled, but now feel uncertain. Third, you feel mentally scattered in a way that makes it hard to focus during prayer or to hold a clear thought about your assignment for more than a few minutes. When all three of those things are happening together, that's not a season of spiritual dryness. That's the Ashdodite spirit attacking your mind gate.

The weapon against this spirit is verbal confession of truth. Not just thinking true thoughts. Speaking them out loud. The reason this matters is rooted in how God designed the spoken word to function in the spirit. When Jesus was in the wilderness and the enemy came at Him with confusion and distortion, He didn't engage in an internal debate. He spoke. "It is written." Three times. Three direct, verbal confessions of the truth of God's Word against the specific distortion the enemy was presenting. He didn't try to out-think the enemy. He out-spoke him. And the enemy left.

That's your model for breaking the Ashdodite spirit. When the fog of confusion comes, you don't sit in it and hope it lifts. You speak truth out loud until the fog breaks.

Specifically, you speak truth about three things: your identity, your assignment, and your ability to hear from God. Here's a specific warfare decree for the Ashdodite spirit that you can speak out loud today: "I decree that I have the mind of Christ according to 1 Corinthians 2:16. I bind every spirit of confusion and mental fog operating against my thinking right now in the name of Jesus. My mind gate is under the blood of Jesus and nothing that brings confusion has legal access to it. I can hear God clearly. I know my assignment. I know who I am. The calling God placed on my life before I was born is still active and still clear, and no spirit of confusion can cloud what heaven has written over me." Speak it out loud. Speak it slowly. Speak it with conviction. The fog doesn't lift because you feel better. It lifts because you spoke truth into it with authority.

There's also a practical discipline for guarding the mind gate against the Ashdodite spirit over the long term. It's the discipline of review. Once a week, sit down with your journal and write out in one or two sentences the specific assignment God has given you right now. Not a theological essay. One or two sentences. The clearer and more specific, the better. Then read it back to yourself out loud. This practice does two things. It keeps your assignment sharp and clear in your own thinking. And it creates a regular checkpoint where you can notice if the Ashdodite spirit has been slowly eroding your clarity without you realizing it. If you sit down to write that one or two sentences and you can't do it, that's a sign. That's when you know the mind gate has been compromised and you need to push back with verbal confession of truth until the clarity returns.

The Ashdodite spirit cannot survive in an atmosphere of consistent, specific, spoken truth. It thrives in silence, in passivity, in the absence of the Word. The more saturated your mind is with the Word of God, the less room this spirit has to operate. Read your Bible out loud. Pray out loud. Decree your assignment out loud. Keep the Word moving through your lips and through the atmosphere around you. That's not just a spiritual discipline. It's a defensive strategy against the spirit that wants to make you forget who you are and what you were sent to do.

Fighting with Both Hands

Nehemiah never came off the wall. That's one of the most important sentences in this entire book. Three spirits came at him. Sanballat brought discouragement. Tobiah brought slander. The Ashdodites brought confusion. All three at the same time. And Nehemiah's response was one of the most practical and powerful pictures of watchman-level intercession in all of Scripture. He told his people to hold a weapon in one hand and a building tool in the other. They built with one hand and fought with the other. And they never stopped building.

That image is your operating model as a *Shamar* watchman. You don't get to choose between building and fighting. You do both. At the same time. Continuously. The building is your assignment, the prayers you pray, the decrees you issue, the people in your *metron* you're pushing forward through the Nehemiah roadmap gate by gate. The fighting is the active resistance of the three spirits that are always working to pull you off your post. You can't put down the building tool to fight. And you can't put down the weapon to build. Both hands are always occupied.

This is what intercession actually looks like in the real world. People sometimes have a picture of the intercessor as someone who lives in a prayer room, removed from the demands of normal life, spending every hour in spiritual warfare. But that's not the Nehemiah model. Nehemiah was managing a massive construction project. He was dealing with logistics, personnel, resources, and opposition all at the same time. He was living a full, demanding life. And he was fighting with one hand while doing all of it. That's the picture of a watchman who has integrated their calling into the fabric of their daily existence rather than separating it out as a special activity reserved for certain hours.

Fighting with both hands also means you've accepted that the fight will never fully stop while you're on the wall. There won't be a season where Sanballat retires and Tobiah gives up and the Ashdodites go home. The three spirits will keep working as long as you're in your assignment. What changes isn't the presence of opposition. What changes is your ability to recognize it quickly, respond to it precisely, and return to building without losing momentum. The goal isn't to reach a place where you're never attacked. The goal is to reach a place where you're never surprised by the attack and never destabilized by it.

There's a passage in Genesis 15 that captures another dimension of this two-handed reality. Abraham built an altar and laid his sacrifice on it. And while he waited, the Bible says vultures came down on the carcasses. They came to steal the sacrifice. And Abraham drove them away. He woke up and he fought. He didn't let the birds take what he had offered to God. That picture is directly applicable to the watchman's life. Every time you build something in the spirit, every time you pray through a gate for someone in your *metron*, every time you issue a decree that shifts something in the atmosphere, the enemy will send something to try to steal what you've built. He'll send discouragement to make you doubt whether the prayer worked. He'll send slander to discredit you before the people you prayed for. He'll send confusion to make you forget what you decreed. And like Abraham, you have to drive the birds away. You have to protect what you've offered. You have to refuse to let the enemy steal the sacrifice of your intercession.

Driving the birds away isn't complicated. It's the same weapon you've already been given. Verbal decree. Specific prayer. The refusal to accept what the enemy is trying to take. When you feel the fruit of your intercession being stolen by discouragement, speak out loud: "I drive away every spirit that's coming to steal what I've built in prayer. My sacrifice stands. My decree stands. What God established through my intercession is sealed in the courts of heaven and no scavenger spirit has access to it." That's not dramatic. That's a watchman protecting their altar the same way Abraham protected his.

The practical rhythm of fighting with both hands looks like this in your daily life. Every morning, before you do anything else, pick up both tools. Spend five minutes reviewing your assignment, the people in your *metron*, the specific things you're building in prayer for each of them. That's picking up the building tool. Then spend five minutes doing a quick spiritual inventory. Ask yourself: which of the three spirits was loudest yesterday? Was it Sanballat, making you feel like your prayers aren't worth the effort? Was it Tobiah, making you preoccupied with what someone said about you? Was it the Ashdodite spirit, clouding your thinking about your calling? Identify which spirit was most active. That's picking up the weapon. Then speak the specific warfare decree for that spirit out loud before you start your day. Build a little. Fight a little. Then go live your life with both tools in your hands.

Nehemiah's builders didn't fight all day and build all day as two separate activities. They did both simultaneously. The weapon was always in reach. The building tool was always in the other hand. They were never fully in one mode or the other. That's the posture of a mature watchman. You're never so focused on the building that you forget the fight is happening. And you're never so consumed by the fight that you stop building. Both hands. Always.

The souls in your sphere are counting on you to stay on the wall. The people in your *metron*, your family, your church, your city, they need a watchman who won't come down. They need someone who has learned to build with one hand and fight with the other, who has named the three spirits and knows how to push back against each one, who refuses to let discouragement or slander or confusion pull them away from the assignment God gave them. That's the *Shamar* anointing in its most mature and practical expression. Not the ability to pray loud or pray long. The ability to stay. To remain. To keep building no matter what comes.

There are too many souls on the line to come off the wall.

Warfare Decrees and Your Next Steps

You now have names for the three spirits that will fight you on the wall. You know what Sanballat sounds like, what Tobiah is after, and how the Ashdodite spirit works. You know Nehemiah's model of fighting with both hands. And you know that the wall being built through your intercession is worth staying on the wall for, no matter how long it takes and no matter what the enemy sends against you.

The recap is simple. Sanballat is the spirit of discouragement. It attacks your motivation and tells you that your prayers aren't producing anything worth the effort. Tobiah is the spirit of slander. It attacks your reputation and works to cut off the people in your sphere from the anointing you carry. The Ashdodite spirit is the spirit of confusion. It attacks your mind gate and clouds your ability to hear clearly from heaven and hold onto the truth of your calling. All three work together with one goal: get you off the wall. And all three are defeated by the same response: stay on the wall, speak truth out loud, and keep building.

Here are your action steps. There are four of them.

The first action step is to identify which of the three voices has been loudest in your life over the past two weeks. Not which one you've heard at some point. Which one has been most consistently active against you recently. Write its name down on a piece of paper. Be honest. That identification is the beginning of your counter-attack.

The second action step is to speak the specific warfare decree for that spirit out loud today. Not tomorrow. Today. If Sanballat has been loudest, speak the decree from the first section of this chapter over yourself right now. If Tobiah has been working against your reputation, speak the decree from the second section. If the Ashdodite spirit has been clouding your thinking, speak the decree from the third section. Speak it out loud, slowly, with conviction. Then write the date next to the name of the spirit you identified. That's your starting point. That's the day you named it and pushed back against it with the authority of the Word of God.

The third action step is to set up the two-handed rhythm in your daily routine starting tomorrow morning. Before you do anything else, spend five minutes reviewing one specific person in your *metron* that you're building in prayer. Then spend five minutes identifying which of the three spirits was most active yesterday in your own life or in the life of that person. Then speak the relevant warfare decree out loud. Five minutes of building. Five minutes of fighting. One decree spoken out loud. That's the whole rhythm. It takes ten minutes. It keeps both hands active. Do it every morning this week and write down in your journal what you notice shifting by the end of the seven days.

The fourth action step is to write out your assignment in one or two specific sentences and read it out loud every morning for the next thirty days. Not a theological statement about intercession in general. Your specific assignment. The people God has given you to guard. The territory He's placed in your care. One or two sentences. Clear. Specific. Spoken out loud. That practice guards your mind gate against the Ashdodite spirit's long-term strategy of slow erosion. It keeps your assignment sharp and present in your thinking every single day. And a watchman who knows exactly what they're guarding and says it out loud every morning is a watchman who doesn't drift off the wall without noticing.

The wall you're building through your intercession is real. The gates you're pushing people through in your sphere are real. The legal decrees you're issuing in the courts of heaven are real. And the three spirits that are working to stop all of it are real. Name them. Fight them. Stay on the wall.

The *Shamar* anointing over your family and your city depends on a watchman who won't come down.

Activation & Reflection

---

1. Where has the spirit of Sanballat (discouragement) most effectively attacked your intercessory life? How did you or will you respond?

____

____

____

____

2. Have you experienced the spirit of Tobiah (slander and accusation) working to stop your prayer assignment? What was the source, and how did you handle it?

____

____

____

____

3. Where has the spirit of the Ashdodite (confusion and spiritual mixture) created compromise or diluted the effectiveness of your prayers?

____

____

____

____

4. How does Nehemiah's approach — arming workers with weapons while they built — apply to your current prayer strategy?

____
____
____
____

5. What specific warfare decrees will you speak over your life this week against these three enemy spirits?

____
____
____
____

A Prayer of Spiritual Warfare

Lord God of armies, I identify and renounce the spirits of discouragement, slander, and confusion that have come against my post. I will not come down from the wall to negotiate with the enemy. I take up the Word of God as my weapon and decree: no weapon formed against my assignment shall prosper. Every tongue of accusation is condemned. The confusion of the enemy has no place in my mind or my ministry. I build and I fight — simultaneously — by Your Spirit. In Jesus' name, Amen.

CHAPTER 10

Creating the Glory Cloud

There's something that happens when a watchman stays faithful to their post long enough. It's not just that their prayers get stronger. It's not just that their spiritual perception sharpens. Something begins to form around them. An atmosphere. A presence. A weight of glory that follows them wherever they go. People feel it before they can explain it. Rooms shift when the watchman walks in. Conversations change. Burdens lift. Breakthroughs happen not because the watchman prayed a specific prayer in that moment, but because of what they've been building in the secret place for weeks and months and years. That's the glory cloud. And it's not reserved for a select few. It's the natural result of a life saturated in the Word and sustained by intimacy with God.

This chapter is about how you build it.

Not just how you experience it occasionally. How you carry it consistently. How you become someone who doesn't just pray for atmospheres but creates them. That's the shift that separates a person who prays from a person who carries the *Shamar* anointing at its fullest expression. And it starts with something that most believers underestimate completely: the cleansing power of the Word of God over the human mind.

Washing with the Word

You've probably heard it said that the blood of Jesus cleanses the heart. That's true. Completely and powerfully true. When you came to Christ, the blood washed away every sin, every stain, every legal accusation the enemy had against you. The heart was cleansed. The record was cleared. But here's what many believers don't fully understand: being saved doesn't automatically clean up your mind. The heart and the mind are two different things. And the enemy knows the difference even when you don't.

Ephesians 5:26 says that Christ sanctifies the church "by the washing of water with the word." That's not talking about salvation. It's talking about sanctification. It's talking about the ongoing process of having your mind cleaned by consistent exposure to the Word of God. The blood handles the heart. The Word handles the mind. Both are necessary. And a watchman who has a clean heart but an unsanctified mind is still vulnerable in ways they may not realize.

Think about what happens when someone gets saved but doesn't get into the Word. Their heart is genuinely changed. Their spirit is born again. But their mind still has the old grooves, the old patterns, the old desires, the old ways of thinking that were shaped by years of living outside of

God. And those old thought patterns give off what could be called a spiritual scent. They attract the same demonic activity that used to have access to that person before they were saved. The person is genuinely born again, but they keep finding themselves surrounded by the same situations, the same temptations, the same people, wondering why nothing has changed. The answer isn't that they're not truly saved. The answer is that their mind hasn't been washed yet.

The priests in the tabernacle understood something about this. In the outer courts, there was a laver of water. Before they could approach the presence of God, they washed. They cleansed their hands, their face, their feet. It was a ceremony of preparation. But there was a limitation to that washing. The only reflection in that water was their own reflection. They could see themselves, but they couldn't be fundamentally changed by what they saw. They could clean the outside, but the inside remained untouched. That's the picture of a believer who goes through religious motions without ever getting into the Word deeply enough for it to do its transforming work.

Jesus changed everything when He said, "I am the living water. Whoever drinks of me will never thirst again." He was speaking to the Samaritan woman at the well in John 4. She was someone whose mind had been shaped by years of broken relationships, compromise, and shame. She came to the well at noon, the hottest part of the day, because she was avoiding people who knew her story. Her heart was open to God, but her mind was still carrying the weight of everything she'd been. And then she encountered the living water. The Word Himself. And something happened in her that no laver of water in any outer court could have produced. Her desires changed. The things she used to want, she didn't want anymore. The men who used to follow her for all the wrong reasons now followed her straight to Jesus. Her atmosphere changed completely. Not because she tried harder. Because her mind was washed.

That's what the Word of God does when you take it seriously as a watchman. It doesn't just inform you. It transforms the atmosphere you carry. It changes what comes out of you. It shifts the spiritual scent of your life from something that attracts darkness to something that repels it. And the more saturated your mind becomes with the Word, the stronger that atmospheric shift becomes. The glory cloud doesn't form in a vacuum. It forms in a mind that's been consistently washed by the Word over time.

Now here's where this becomes very practical for the *Shamar* call. Your mind is a gate. Just like the gates of Jerusalem controlled what came in and out of the city, your mind controls what enters your inner world and what flows out of it into the atmosphere around you. A mind that hasn't been washed by the Word is a gate with gaps in it. Thoughts get through that shouldn't. Patterns establish themselves that don't belong. And the spiritual atmosphere around you reflects what's getting through the gate. But a mind that's been washed by the Word becomes a gate that's tight and secure. The scent it gives off is the scent of Christ. And that scent creates an atmosphere that the enemy can't penetrate and that people in your sphere are drawn toward without always knowing why.

There's a specific process for using the Word as a cleansing agent that goes beyond just reading a devotional in the morning. It requires intentionality. It requires what could be called active washing rather than passive exposure. Here's exactly what that looks like in practice.

The first step is to read the Word out loud. Not silently. Out loud. There's a reason this matters. Romans 10:17 says faith comes by hearing, and hearing by the Word of God. The ear gate is one of the primary pathways through which the Word does its cleansing work. When you speak the Word out loud, you're sending it through your own ear gate. You're hearing it with your own ears. And what goes in through the ear gate begins to displace what was already sitting in the mind. Thoughts that contradict what God says about you can't survive long in a mind that's consistently hearing the Word spoken out loud. The truth crowds out the lie. The living water pushes out the stagnant water. But it has to go through the ear gate to do it.

The second step is to identify the specific area of your mind that needs the most washing right now. Not in general. Specifically. Is it the way you think about your worth and your identity? Is it fear-based thinking that keeps pulling your prayer life into anxiety rather than authority? Is it old patterns of desire that still surface even though you've been saved for years? Name it. Write it down. Then find the specific scriptures that speak directly to that area and read them out loud every day for thirty days. Not once. Every day. Thirty days. That's not a ritual. That's a washing cycle. You're running the Word through the gate of your mind repeatedly until the old thought pattern no longer has the grip it used to have.

The third step is to declare your home a sanctified atmosphere after your washing time. This is where the *Shamar* anointing connects directly to the glory cloud. After you've spent time reading the Word out loud and washing your mind, stand up and speak out loud over your home. Say something like this: "In the name of Jesus, I declare that this home is a zone of the glory cloud. The atmosphere of this house is sanctified by the Word of God and the blood of Jesus. Nothing that opposes the presence of God has legal access to this space. The glory of the Lord fills this home. This is a place where the enemy cannot penetrate and where the presence of God is welcome and active." That's not just a nice prayer. That's a watchman using the *Shamar* call to govern the atmosphere of their own home through the Word and through decree. You're doing exactly what God designed you to do in Genesis 2:15 when He told Adam to keep and guard the garden. You're keeping and guarding your atmosphere.

Consider a hypothetical scenario to make this tangible. Think about a woman named Ketura, a 42-year-old intercessor who has been saved for fifteen years but has been struggling with a persistent pattern of anxious thinking. She prays. She believes. But her mind keeps defaulting to worst-case scenarios about her children, her finances, her church. She's been to the altar. She's asked God to take the anxiety. But nothing seems to stick for more than a few days. What Ketura doesn't realize is that her mind gate hasn't been consistently washed. She gets into the Word occasionally, but not with the intentionality of someone who knows they're washing a specific area of their thinking. When someone teaches her the principle of washing with the Word, she picks Philippians 4:6-8 as her washing scripture. Every morning for thirty days, she reads it out loud. She speaks it over her mind specifically. She declares her home a zone of the peace of God. By day twenty-two, she notices that the anxious thoughts are arriving less frequently. By day thirty, the pattern has shifted in a way that years of occasional prayer never produced. Her mind gate is cleaner. And the atmosphere in her home has changed. Her children feel it. Her husband comments on it. The glory cloud is forming. Not because of a dramatic spiritual encounter. Because of thirty days of consistent washing.

The enemy doesn't need to get inside you if he can infiltrate your atmosphere. That's one of the most important things a watchman needs to understand about spiritual protection. What you watch, what you listen to, what you allow to stay in your home, what conversations you permit to happen in your space, all of it affects the atmosphere. All of it affects the spiritual scent you give off. All of it either contributes to the glory cloud or compromises it. This isn't about being rigid or religious. It's about being intentional. A watchman who understands that their atmosphere is a weapon will guard it with the same seriousness that Nehemiah guarded the walls of Jerusalem. Because the glory cloud that forms through a washed mind and a guarded atmosphere is one of the most powerful forces available to a *Shamar* watchman. It's what makes your presence in a room carry weight before you say a word. It's what makes people encounter the presence of God simply by being near you.

The Word is the living water. Drink it daily. Speak it out loud. Let it wash the mind gate. And watch what forms around your life as a result.

The Elijah Atmosphere

First Kings 18 gives us one of the most powerful pictures of atmosphere creation in the entire Bible. And it's a picture that every watchman needs to sit with until they fully understand what Elijah was actually doing on Mount Carmel that day.

The situation was dire. Israel had been in a severe drought for three years. The prophets of Baal were on the scene, four hundred and fifty of them, cutting themselves and crying out to a god who couldn't answer. Elijah stood alone on the other side. And then he did something that looked completely counterproductive to everyone watching. He asked for water. He poured it on the altar. Not once. Three times. Until the water ran down and filled the trench around the altar. To any natural observer, this was the worst possible strategy. You don't try to light a fire on a soaking wet altar. You don't pour water on what you need to burn.

But Elijah wasn't praying for fire. He was building an atmosphere.

When fire fell from heaven and hit that water-soaked altar, something happened in the natural that carried a profound spiritual significance. The water evaporated. It rose into the atmosphere. And when water enters the atmosphere in sufficient quantity, it forms a cloud. Elijah wasn't praying for rain and then hoping a cloud would show up. He was creating the conditions for the cloud through his act of faith and sacrifice. He was generating the atmosphere before the manifestation arrived. Then he sent his servant seven times to look for the cloud. Not to look for rain. To look for the cloud that Elijah had already formed through what he'd done on the altar. And on the seventh trip, the servant came back and said he saw a cloud the size of a man's hand rising from the sea. Elijah said run. Because the atmosphere I've already created is about to produce the rain.

That's the picture of a watchman who carries atmosphere rather than praying for it.

There's a distinction here that changes everything about how you understand your role. Most believers approach breakthrough by asking God to send it. They pray for an atmosphere of revival. They cry out for a cloud of glory. They ask God to move in their church, in their city, in their family. And those prayers aren't wrong. But a *Shamar* watchman who understands the Elijah principle doesn't just pray for the cloud. They create it. They build the altar. They pour the water. They do the act of faith and sacrifice that generates the atmosphere. And then they watch what God does with what they've built.

The cloud you carry is formed by what you do in the secret place. Every time you get into the Word and let it wash your mind, you're pouring water on the altar. Every time you spend time in genuine worship before God, you're building the conditions for the cloud. Every time you issue a righteous decree from the courts of heaven, you're adding to what's forming in the atmosphere around your life. The cloud doesn't appear overnight. It's built. It's accumulated. It's the result of consistent, faithful, altar-building over time. But when it's formed, it's real. It's tangible. And it goes with you wherever you go.

This is why Elijah's servant had to look seven times. Seven is the number of completion in Scripture. The fullness of what Elijah had built wasn't visible after one trip. Or two. Or three. It took seven. That's a picture of the patience required to carry an atmosphere rather than just pray for one. The watchman who builds their cloud through consistent intimacy with God doesn't see it fully formed after one week of washing with the Word or one month of worship. It forms over time. It accumulates. And when it reaches its fullness, it produces rain. It produces breakthrough. It produces exactly what God designed it to produce. But you have to keep sending your servant to look. You have to keep building even when all you see is a cloud the size of a man's hand. Because that small cloud is evidence that the altar is working.

Watchmen govern atmospheres. That's not a statement about spiritual superiority. It's a statement about function. God designed the *Shamar* watchman to create and carry a specific kind of spiritual environment that affects everyone who comes near it. The Samaritan woman carried an atmosphere after her encounter with the living water. The men who used to follow her for her body now followed her to Jesus. She didn't try to create that effect. She didn't strategize about how to draw people to God. She simply went back into her city carrying what she'd received at the well. And the atmosphere she carried did the work. People were drawn to what was on her. That's what happens when the glory cloud is real in someone's life. It's not performative. It's not manufactured. It's the natural overflow of a life that's been washed by the Word and sustained by intimacy with God.

Now here's the specific practice for building the Elijah atmosphere in your life. There are seven Hebrew words for praise and worship that function as distinct tools for cloud-building. Each one does something specific in the spirit. You need to know all seven and use them deliberately.

The first is *Barak*. It means to bow down or kneel in reverence and submission to God. This is the posture of bringing your body into alignment with your spirit. When you barak before God, you're physically positioning yourself in submission. You're commanding your flesh to yield. There has to be a moment in your day where you physically bow before God, even if it's just for a few minutes. Not as a ritual. As a genuine act of submission that says, "I am not in charge here. You are." That posture opens the atmosphere for everything that follows.

The second is *Yada*. It means to lift up your hands and confess the sovereignty of God. When you yada, you're throwing your hands up in an act of surrender and acknowledgment. You're declaring with your body that He is sovereign over everything in your life. This isn't just an emotional expression. It's a spiritual positioning that says the Lord is above every circumstance you're facing.

The third is *Todah*. It means to lift your hands in thanksgiving and admiration. Where yada confesses sovereignty, todah expresses gratitude and wonder. It's the act of lifting your hands specifically in thanks, not for what God is going to do, but for who He already is. *Todah* builds an atmosphere of gratitude that repels the spirit of heaviness and invites the spirit of praise.

The fourth is *Shabach*. It means to shout and proclaim the testimony of God. There's a time for quiet, meditative prayer. And there's a time to open your mouth and shout. *Shabach* is that time. When Israel shouted at Jericho, the walls fell. When Paul and Silas sang loudly in the prison, the chains broke. *Shabach* is the tool of vocal proclamation, the act of declaring the testimony of God out loud with volume and conviction. Don't underestimate what a genuine shout of praise does to the atmosphere around you.

The fifth is *Halal*. This is where we get the word hallelujah. It means to boast, to celebrate, to praise God with abandon and without restraint. David halal-ed before the ark of the Lord. The Bible says he danced with all his might. His wife Michal thought it was undignified. But David understood something she didn't. He was building a cloud. He was creating an atmosphere of glory through his uninhibited celebration of God. *Halal* doesn't care what it looks like to observers. It's not performed for people. It's poured out before God. And it generates something in the spirit that careful, controlled worship never touches.

The sixth is *Zamar*. It means to sing, to play music, to make melody before the Lord. You don't have to be a gifted singer for zamar to work. The Bible says make a joyful noise. Not a perfect noise. A joyful one. The spirit of worship that zamar builds in your life is one of the primary protections against spiritual dryness. When the enemy wants to kill your cloud, one of his most effective tactics is killing your desire to sing. When you notice that you don't want to worship, that's exactly when you need to zamar the most. Push through the dryness. Sing anyway. Make the joyful noise even when it doesn't feel joyful yet. The act of zamar creates the atmosphere that the feeling eventually follows.

The seventh is *Tehillah.* It means to sing spontaneously back to God what He's putting in your heart. Not a song from a playlist. Not a hymn from memory. A spontaneous, unrehearsed expression of what the Holy Spirit is placing in you in that moment. David did this throughout the Psalms. He would take what God was speaking to his heart and sing it back. "You are a shield for me, my glory, the lifter of my head." That's tehillah. It's the most intimate form of worship because it's a two-way conversation expressed through song. When you tehillah, you're not just praising God. You're responding to what He's saying. And that level of intimacy is one of the most powerful cloud-building activities available to a watchman.

Using all seven of these tools isn't something you do in one prayer session. But over the course of a week, all seven should show up somewhere in your worship life. Bowing in barak. Lifting hands in yada and todah. Shouting in shabach. Celebrating in halal. Singing in zamar. Responding spontaneously in tehillah. Each one adds a layer to the cloud you're building. Each one contributes to the atmosphere that forms around your life over time. And as the cloud builds, it becomes something you carry with you rather than something you have to manufacture in the moment.

Once the cloud is formed, you have to protect it. This is something Solomon learned when the glory filled the temple. When Solomon finished building the temple and the glory of God came down so powerfully that the priests couldn't even stand to minister, the response wasn't just celebration. It was protection. David had already taught the priests how to guard the glory. Because glory that's unprotected can be lost. An atmosphere that's been built through faithful worship and the Word can be compromised by what you allow into your life and your space. What you watch. What you listen to. What conversations you permit. What spiritual influences you allow to stay close to you. All of it affects the cloud. A watchman who builds their atmosphere carefully but guards it carelessly will find it thinning over time without understanding why.

Guard what you've built with the same seriousness you brought to building it. The glory cloud over your life is a weapon in the *Shamar* anointing. It's what makes your presence in a room carry weight. It's what creates the conditions for breakthrough in the lives of the people you're assigned to guard. Protect it. Maintain it. And keep building it, day by day, through the Word and through worship, until it becomes the defining feature of the atmosphere you carry wherever you go.

Recap and Action Steps

The glory cloud is not a mystical experience reserved for a few unusually spiritual people. It's the natural result of two specific things working together: a mind that's been consistently washed by the Word and a life that's been sustained by genuine, deliberate intimacy with God through worship. The blood cleanses the heart. The Word cleanses the mind. And a clean mind, saturated in the Word and expressed through worship, forms a cloud that the enemy cannot penetrate and that people in your sphere are drawn toward without always knowing why.

Elijah didn't pray for the cloud. He created it through his sacrifice and his act of faith on Mount Carmel. You create yours through the daily discipline of washing your mind with the Word and building your altar through the seven Hebrew expressions of worship. The cloud forms over time. It accumulates. And when it reaches its fullness, it produces rain. It produces breakthrough. It produces exactly what God designed it to produce in the lives of the people you're called to guard.

Your action steps for this chapter are specific and they build on each other. Do them in order.

The first action step is to begin a thirty-day washing cycle starting today. Identify one specific area of your mind that needs the most cleansing right now. Not in general. One specific area. Fear. Old desires. Anxious thinking. Discouragement about your calling. Whatever it is, name it. Then find two or three scriptures that speak directly to that area. Write them on an index card or in your phone. Read them out loud every morning for thirty days. Not as a ritual. As a washing. Speak them slowly. Let them go through your ear gate. Speak them over your mind specifically. Say, "God, I'm washing my mind with your Word right now in this area.

I'm applying the living water to the gate of my thinking. Let your Word do what the blood did for my heart."

The second action step is to declare your home a zone of the glory cloud every day this week after your washing time. After you've read the Word out loud and washed your mind, stand up, speak out loud over your home, and declare it a sanctified atmosphere. Use your own words. Make it specific to your home and your family. Speak it with the authority of a *Shamar* watchman who knows they've been assigned to guard the atmosphere of that space. Do this every day for seven days and write down in your journal what you observe shifting in the atmosphere of your home during that week.

The third action step is to incorporate all seven Hebrew expressions of worship into your prayer life this week. You don't have to do all seven in one sitting. Assign one or two to each day. Monday, practice barak and yada. Tuesday, todah and shabach. Wednesday, halal. Thursday, zamar. Friday, tehillah. Give each one at least five minutes of genuine, focused expression. Not performance. Genuine worship using that specific tool. At the end of the week, write down which one felt most natural and which one felt most uncomfortable. The one that felt most uncomfortable is likely the one that will produce the most significant breakthrough in your cloud-building. Lean into it next week.

The fourth action step is to identify one thing in your life that's been compromising your atmosphere and make a decision about it today. Not a vague intention to be more careful. A specific, named thing. A specific show you've been watching that leaves a spiritual residue. A specific conversation you've been allowing that brings the wrong atmosphere into your space. A specific habit that's been thinning the cloud you're trying to build. Name it. Decide what you're going to do about it. Write it down. And act on that decision today. Protecting the cloud is as important as building it. A watchman who builds carefully but guards carelessly will lose what they worked to create. Identify the gap and close it.

The *Shamar* anointing over your family and your city is carried in the atmosphere you build and maintain through the Word and through worship. The cloud you create in the secret place is the weapon you carry into every room, every relationship, every spiritual battle. Build it faithfully. Guard it intentionally. And watch what God does with the atmosphere of a watchman who has stayed on the wall long enough for the cloud to form.

Activation & Reflection

---

1. Have you ever experienced the tangible manifest presence of God in corporate or personal prayer? Describe what happened and what preceded it.

____

____

____

____

2. What specific worship and intercession practices most consistently position you to experience God's glory?

____

____

____

____

3. What hinders the glory cloud from resting on your personal life and on your church or prayer community?

____

____

____

____

4. How does the marriage of worship and intercession differ from prayer alone? What shifts in the atmosphere when you add extravagant praise?

____

____

____

____

5. What practical steps will you take this week to create the conditions for the glory cloud to rest on your life and your community?

____

____

____

____

A Prayer for the Glory Cloud

Holy Spirit, I invite Your manifest presence to rest upon my life, my home, and my church. I create an atmosphere of praise and intercession for Your glory to inhabit. Consume everything that is merely religious and replace it with living fire. Let the glory cloud settle on my altar of prayer. I am not content with information about You — I hunger for an encounter with You. Come, Lord, and fill this place. In Jesus' name, Amen.

CHAPTER 11

The Seven Hebrew Praises

Worship is a weapon. Most believers know that on some level, but they've never been taught exactly how the weapon works. They sing on Sunday. They lift their hands when the music moves them. They shout when the Spirit falls. But they've never understood that each of those expressions carries a specific function in the spirit. They're not interchangeable. They're not just different flavors of the same thing. Each one of the seven Hebrew words for praise does something distinct in the atmosphere. Each one is a specific tool designed to accomplish a specific purpose. And a *Shamar* watchman who doesn't know how to use all seven is like a builder who only knows how to use one tool no matter what the job requires.

The glory cloud you read about in the last chapter doesn't form by accident. It forms through deliberate, intentional worship using the right expressions at the right time. And the more you understand what each expression actually does in the spirit, the more precise you become in using it. You stop praising randomly and start praising strategically. Not because worship is a formula, but because God designed these seven expressions to do specific things, and knowing what they do changes how you approach them.

This chapter is going to break all seven down. Not just their definitions, but their functions. Not just what they mean, but what they accomplish when you use them in the context of the *Shamar* call. Because the watchman who knows how to use praise as a tactical weapon doesn't just build atmosphere. They shift atmospheres. They break things that warfare prayer alone couldn't touch. They establish the throne of God in spaces where the enemy thought he had a foothold. And they do it through worship, through the seven ancient expressions that God designed to govern the spiritual atmosphere over every territory a watchman has been assigned to guard.

Barack and *Yada*: Submission and Sovereignty

The flesh doesn't want to bow. That's the first thing you need to understand about *Barak.* Your flesh wants to stand, to assert itself, to remain in control. Kneeling is a posture that the flesh resists instinctively. And that's exactly why it's so powerful.

Barak is the Hebrew word that means to kneel, to bow down, to bless God from a posture of reverence and submission. It's used in Psalm 95:6 where it says, "Come, let us bow down in worship, let us kneel before the Lord our Maker." The physical act of kneeling isn't just ceremonial.

It's a declaration. When you physically bring your body into submission before God, something happens in the spirit that doesn't happen when you stay standing. The flesh is commanded to yield. The self is put in its proper place. And the spirit, now free from the resistance of a body that wants to remain in charge, can connect with heaven at a different level.

There's a reason so many believers live in what could be called "head prayer." They pray from the neck up. Their mind is engaged, their words are flowing, but their body is completely uninvolved. They're sitting comfortably, or standing casually, or lying in bed, and they're talking to God without any physical engagement with what they're saying. And the result is prayer that feels disconnected. Prayer that doesn't seem to land. Prayer that stays in the realm of thought rather than moving into the realm of spirit. *Barak* is the remedy for head prayer. It brings the whole body into the act of worship. It makes your physical posture agree with what your spirit is declaring.

When you kneel before God, you're doing something that carries legal weight in the spirit. You're physically enacting the truth that He is sovereign and you are not. You're putting your body in the position of a servant before a King. And that act of physical submission breaks the power of the flesh over your prayer life in a way that mental agreement alone never accomplishes. Paul said in Romans 8:13 that if you live according to the flesh, you will die, but if by the Spirit you put to death the deeds of the body, you will live. *Barak* is one of the ways you put the body in its place. Not through punishment, but through posture. You kneel, and the flesh loses its grip on the atmosphere.

Here's the specific practice for *Barak*. Once a day, at the beginning of your prayer time, physically kneel. Not in your chair. On the floor. If your knees allow it, get all the way down. If not, kneel as fully as your body permits. Then say out loud: "Lord, I bring my body before you in submission right now. I am not in charge. You are. My flesh does not rule this prayer time. Your Spirit does. I bow before you as my King, my Maker, and my God." Hold that position for at least two minutes before you say anything else. Don't rush past it. Let the posture do its work. Let the flesh yield. Let your spirit come into alignment with the truth your body is declaring. Then pray from that place. You'll notice a difference in the quality of your connection with heaven when you've entered through *Barak* rather than just sitting down and starting to talk.

The second Hebrew word in this section is *Yada*. Where *Barak* is about kneeling, *Yada* is about lifting. It means to throw up your hands in an open act of confession and surrender, specifically confessing the sovereignty of God. The root of the word carries the idea of extending your hands outward and upward, not just raising them politely, but throwing them up in an act of total acknowledgment that God is above everything you're facing.

Yada is the word behind the phrase "give thanks to the Lord" in Psalm 107:1. But it's not just gratitude. It's a confession of His supremacy. When you yada, you're declaring with your body and your voice that He is above every circumstance, every problem, every attack, every disappointment, every situation that's been pressing in on your life. You're physically enacting the truth that He is higher than all of it. Your hands going up is your body saying, "I surrender control. You are sovereign. I confess that you are above everything I've been carrying."

For a *Shamar* watchman, *Yada* is especially important in seasons of spiritual pressure. When you're under attack from the three spirits on the wall, when discouragement is loud and confusion is thick and the slander of Tobiah is ringing in your ears, the act of throwing your hands up in *Yada* is one of the most powerful things you can do. You're not surrendering to the enemy. You're surrendering control to God. You're confessing that He is sovereign over everything the enemy is trying to use against you. And that confession, made with your whole body, shifts something in the atmosphere that words alone don't shift.

Together, *Barak* and *Yada* form the foundation of what it means to bring your full body into submission before God. One brings you down. The other lifts you up. One commands the flesh to yield. The other confesses the sovereignty of the One you're yielding to. They work together as the opening posture of a watchman who understands that prayer is not just a mental activity. It's a full-body act of spiritual positioning. When you've knelt in *Barak* and thrown your hands up in *Yada*, you've already done something in the spirit before you've said a single word of intercession. You've established who is in charge. You've aligned your body with your spirit. And you've created the conditions for everything else that follows to carry more weight.

Think about a hypothetical scenario to make this real. Consider a man named Elias, a 40-year-old intercessor who has been standing in the gap for his prodigal daughter for two years. He prays faithfully. He decrees. He builds his case in the courts of heaven. But lately his prayer time has felt mechanical. He's going through the motions, saying the right things, but not feeling the connection. He hasn't changed his words. He hasn't changed his content. But he's been praying from his couch, casually, without any physical engagement. When someone teaches him about *Barak* and *Yada*, he tries it. He gets on his knees on the floor of his bedroom. He throws his hands up and confesses God's sovereignty over his daughter's life out loud. Something breaks in the room. Not because the words were different. Because his body finally joined the prayer. The flesh yielded. The atmosphere shifted. And the quality of his intercession that morning was unlike anything he'd experienced in months. The posture unlocked the presence.

The action step for this section is specific. For the next seven days, begin every single prayer time with *Barak* and *Yada*. Kneel first. Hold it for two minutes in silence. Then throw your hands up and speak your confession of God's sovereignty out loud, specifically naming the things in your life and your *metron* that you're placing under His authority. Do it before you pray anything else. Before your list. Before your decrees. Before your intercession. Let the posture establish the atmosphere. Then pray from that place. Keep a journal of what shifts in your prayer life over those seven days. The difference will be noticeable.

Shabak and *Halel*: The Shout and the Foolish Dance

There's a reason the enemy works so hard to make worship dignified.

If he can keep your praise contained, controlled, and quiet, he can limit its impact. Because the two expressions of worship in this section, *Shabach* and *Halal*, are specifically designed to break things that quiet, controlled worship doesn't touch. They're high-energy. They're loud. They're uninhibited. And they confuse the enemy in a way that nothing else does.

Shabach means to shout, to address in a loud tone, to proclaim the testimony and the victory of God with volume and conviction. It's not a gentle expression. It's the shout of someone who has seen what God has done and can't contain their proclamation of it. You see it in Psalm 117:1, "Praise the Lord, all you nations. Extol him, all you peoples." That word "extol" is *Shabach*. It's a command to shout His praise. Not suggest it. Not whisper it. Shout it.

When Israel shouted at Jericho, the walls fell. When Paul and Silas sang loudly in the prison at midnight, the chains broke and the doors flew open. When Jehoshaphat sent the worshippers out in front of the army shouting praise, God set ambushes against the enemy and the battle was won before the soldiers ever drew a sword. There's a pattern in Scripture that's impossible to miss. Vocal, loud, declared praise does something in the spirit that silent prayer doesn't do. It releases something. It breaks something. It confuses the enemy's strategy in a way that he simply can't counter, because the atmosphere of declared praise is the one environment where darkness cannot hold its ground.

Shabach is tactical. When you shout the testimony of God, when you declare out loud what He has done and who He is, you're doing two things simultaneously. You're building up your own faith by hearing the testimony come out of your own mouth. And you're releasing a sound into the spirit realm that the enemy has no defense against. He can counter your arguments. He can counter your questions. He can counter your doubts. But he cannot counter the sound of a watchman shouting the testimony of God with genuine conviction. That sound is a weapon. And the *Shamar* watchman who learns to use it will break things in the atmosphere over their family and their city that years of quiet petition never moved.

Now here's the specific practice for *Shabach*. Once a week, set aside fifteen minutes specifically for this expression. Find a place where you can be loud without worrying about disturbing others. Stand up. Don't sit. Standing is the posture of proclamation. Then shout the testimony of God over your specific *metron*. Not a general shout of praise. A specific, targeted, loud proclamation of what God has done and is doing in the lives of the people He's assigned to you. Shout it over your children by name. Shout it over your church. Shout it over your city. "God is moving in my son's life right now. I shout the testimony of His faithfulness over him. I declare that what God started He will finish. I shout the victory of Jesus Christ over every assignment of the enemy against this family." That's *Shabach*. That's the shout of testimony as a tactical weapon. Do it until you feel the atmosphere shift. You'll know when it does. There's a specific sense of breakthrough that follows genuine *Shabach* that's unlike anything else in your worship toolkit.

Halal is where things get uncomfortable for most believers. And that discomfort is exactly the point.

Halal is the root of the word "hallelujah." It means to boast in God, to celebrate Him with abandon and without restraint, to praise Him in a way that looks foolish to observers. The word itself carries the idea of shining, of making a show, of celebrating so freely that dignity goes out the window. David halal-ed before the ark of the Lord when it was being brought into Jerusalem. The Bible says he danced with all his might, leaping and whirling before the Lord. He was so uninhibited in his celebration that his wife Michal looked out the window and despised him for it. She thought it was undignified for a king. But David's response to her criticism is one of the most powerful statements about *Halal* in all of Scripture. He said, "I will be even more undignified than this."

David understood something that Michal didn't. *Halal* isn't about performance. It's not about how it looks to people watching. It's a specific spiritual act of celebration directed entirely at God, and it carries a power that careful, controlled worship cannot access. The spirit of heaviness, which Isaiah 61:3 specifically identifies as something that praise is designed to break, cannot survive in the atmosphere of genuine *Halal*. You can't be heavy and halal at the same time. The two are spiritually incompatible. When you choose to celebrate God with total abandon, regardless of how it looks or how you feel, the spirit of heaviness has to go. It has no legal ground in an atmosphere of uninhibited praise.

For the *Shamar* watchman, *Halal* is one of the most powerful tools for breaking spiritual atmospheres over assigned territory. When you feel the weight of a heavy assignment, when the burden of intercession for a specific person or situation has been pressing on you for a long time, when the atmosphere over your home or your church feels thick and resistant, that's when you need to *Halal*. Not when you feel like it. Especially when you don't. The choice to celebrate God foolishly in the face of a heavy atmosphere is an act of spiritual warfare that confuses the enemy, breaks the heaviness, and shifts the atmosphere in a way that nothing else does.

The enemy's strategy against watchmen isn't always direct confrontation. Sometimes it's just weight. Just heaviness. Just the slow, grinding pressure of carrying a burden that never seems to lift. And the weapon against that strategy is exactly what the enemy doesn't expect: joy. Celebration. Foolish, uninhibited, undignified praise that says, "I'm not going to be defined by this weight. I choose to celebrate my God right now in the middle of it." That choice is a declaration of faith. It's a decree that the weight doesn't have the final word. And it creates an atmosphere that the enemy simply cannot operate in.

The specific practice for *Halal* is this. Once this week, choose the most uncomfortable form of celebration you can think of and do it before God in your private space. If dancing feels foolish to you, dance. If shouting feels undignified, shout. If spinning around with your hands in the air looks ridiculous to you, do it. The point isn't the specific action. The point is the choice to be undignified before God. To let go of the self-consciousness that keeps your praise contained. To celebrate Him with your whole body in a way that your flesh finds embarrassing. That's *Halal*. And the breakthrough it produces in the atmosphere over your life will be worth every moment of discomfort your flesh experienced in the process.

Shabach and *Halal* together form the high-energy dimension of the watchman's praise toolkit. One is the shout of testimony. The other is the dance of celebration. Together, they create an atmospheric environment that confuses the enemy's strategy, breaks the spirit of heaviness, and establishes the joy of the Lord as the dominant spiritual reality over your assigned territory. They're not optional extras for believers who like that kind of thing. They're tactical weapons that the *Shamar* watchman deploys deliberately and strategically as part of the work of guarding the atmosphere over their family and their city.

Zamar and *Tehillah*: Instrumental and Spontaneous Song

Music is older than the church. It's older than Israel. It goes back to the very nature of heaven itself. In Job 38:7, God describes the morning stars singing together when He laid the foundations of the earth. Before the first human voice ever lifted in worship, there was song in the presence of God. Music isn't a cultural add-on to spiritual life. It's woven into the fabric of how heaven operates. And the two Hebrew expressions in this section, *Zamar* and *Tehillah*, give the *Shamar* watchman access to dimensions of the spirit that the other five expressions of praise don't reach.

Zamar means to sing, to play a musical instrument, to make melody before the Lord. It's used throughout the Psalms as a call to musical worship. Psalm 47:6 says, "Sing praises to God, sing praises. Sing praises to our King, sing praises." Every use of "sing praises" in that verse is the word zamar. It's a command to make music before God, with voice and with instrument, as an act of intentional worship. The word itself carries the idea of plucking strings, of making a specific musical sound that reaches into the spirit realm in a way that spoken words alone don't.

Music has a unique ability to cultivate the spirit of prophecy. This is something that the watchmen and prophets of the Old Testament understood well. In 2 Kings 3:15, the prophet Elisha called for a musician. The Bible says that as the musician played, the hand of the Lord came upon Elisha and he prophesied. The music created the conditions for the prophetic. It opened a channel in the spirit that allowed God to speak. This isn't mystical or strange. It's the function that *Zamar* was designed to perform. Musical worship cultivates an atmosphere where the prophetic voice of God can be heard more clearly. It quiets the noise of the natural world and tunes the spirit to the frequency of heaven.

For a *Shamar* watchman, *Zamar* is an essential tool for maintaining the spirit of prophecy in your prayer life. If you play an instrument, use it in your worship time specifically as a prophetic tool, not just as a musical performance, but as a deliberate act of creating the conditions for God to speak. Play before Him and then listen. Let the music be the environment in which you wait for His voice. If you don't play an instrument, use recorded music intentionally. Not as background noise while you do other things. As a focused act of *Zamar*, where you're actively participating in the worship, singing along, engaging with the melody as a spiritual act of creating an atmosphere where God can speak.

The specific practice for *Zamar* is this. Three times this week, set aside twenty minutes specifically for musical worship. Choose music that carries the Word of God in its lyrics. Sing along out loud. If you play an instrument, incorporate it. After fifteen minutes of active *Zamar*, stop the music and sit in silence for five minutes. Ask God one specific question about your assigned territory. Write down whatever comes. That five minutes of silence after *Zamar* is often where the clearest prophetic impressions come. Because the music created the atmosphere and the silence gives you space to receive what the atmosphere produced. Do this consistently and you'll find that your prophetic perception about the people in your *metron* sharpens significantly over time.

Tehillah is the most intimate of all seven expressions. It means to sing spontaneously, to give forth a new song, to sing back to God what He is putting in your heart in the moment. It's not a rehearsed song. It's not a song from a playlist. It's a live, unrehearsed, Spirit-led expression of what God is speaking to your spirit right now. David's Psalms are full of tehillah. He would take what God was saying to him and sing it back. "You are a shield for me, my glory, the lifter of my head." That's not a performance. That's a conversation set to melody. It's the most direct form of two-way communication with God that worship offers.

Psalm 22:3 says that God inhabits the praises of His people. The word "praises" in that verse is tehillah. God doesn't just attend your worship. He inhabits it. He takes up residence in the spontaneous song that rises from a heart that's genuinely responding to what He's saying. When you tehillah, you're not just worshipping God. You're creating a dwelling place for His presence. You're building something in the spirit that He actually lives in. And a watchman who carries that kind of presence doesn't just pray for atmospheres. They become an atmosphere. Everywhere they go, people encounter the God who inhabits their praise.

For many believers, *Tehillah* feels the most intimidating of the seven expressions. It requires you to open your mouth and sing something you haven't prepared. Something unrehearsed. Something that might sound imperfect or awkward. And that vulnerability is exactly what makes it so powerful. Because *Tehillah* isn't about musical quality. It's about spiritual authenticity. God isn't grading your pitch. He's responding to the sincerity of a heart that's willing to be vulnerable enough to sing what He's putting there, even if it sounds simple, even if it's just a few repeated phrases, even if no one else would find it impressive.

The specific practice for *Tehillah* is this. After your next time of *Zamar*, after you've sung along with worship music and created the atmosphere, transition into silence. Then open your mouth and sing whatever comes. Don't think about it. Don't plan it. Just sing what's in your heart in that moment. It might be one phrase repeated over and over. It might be a scripture set to a simple melody. It might be just a few words. Don't judge it. Don't edit it. Let it flow. That's *Tehillah*. And as you practice it consistently, the spontaneous song will come more easily. The Holy Spirit will have more to work with as your mind gets washed by the Word and your spirit becomes more sensitive to His voice. Over time, your *Tehillah* will become one of the most powerful tools in your cloud-building practice. Because the song God puts in you is the song that carries His presence. And the presence you carry is the atmosphere that guards your family, your church, and your city.

Zamar and *Tehillah* together form the musical dimension of the watchman's worship. One is intentional, structured musical worship that cultivates the prophetic. The other is spontaneous, Spirit-led song that creates a dwelling place for God's presence. Together, they build a consistent cloud of glory that forms over the life of a watchman who uses them regularly. They connect the worship life to the prophetic life. They create the conditions for God to speak and for the watchman to hear. And they produce an atmosphere of presence that the enemy cannot penetrate and that the people in your sphere are drawn toward, often without understanding why.

Putting It Into Practice

Seven expressions. Seven tools. Each one designed to accomplish something specific in the spirit. *Barak* brings your body into submission and breaks the power of the flesh over your prayer life. *Yada* confesses the sovereignty of God with your whole body and positions you under His authority.

Shabach releases the shout of testimony that breaks things in the atmosphere that quiet prayer doesn't touch. *Halal* celebrates God with total abandon, breaking the spirit of heaviness and confusing the enemy's strategy. *Zamar* uses music to cultivate the spirit of prophecy and sharpen your ability to hear from heaven. *Tehillah* creates a dwelling place for God's presence through spontaneous, Spirit-led song. Together, they form the complete toolkit of a *Shamar* watchman who uses praise as a strategic weapon in the work of guarding the atmosphere over their assigned territory.

The enemy doesn't want you to use all seven. He wants you to stay in one or two that feel comfortable and ignore the rest. He wants your praise to stay contained, predictable, and safe. Because contained praise doesn't build clouds. It doesn't break atmospheres. It doesn't confuse his strategy. But a watchman who moves through all seven expressions with intentionality and faith becomes someone whose worship is a genuine threat to every assignment the enemy has over their *metron*.

Your action steps are three. Not five. Not seven. Three specific things that you can do starting today.

The first action step is to identify which of the seven expressions feels the most uncomfortable to your flesh right now. Not which one you like the least intellectually. Which one your body and your self-consciousness resist the most. Is it the physical kneeling of *Barak*? The throwing up of hands in *Yada*? The loud shout of *Shabach*? The foolish dance of *Halal*? The spontaneous song of *Tehillah*? Name it. Write it down. That expression is your assignment for this week. The one that feels most uncomfortable to your flesh is the one that will produce the most significant atmospheric shift when you choose to do it anyway. Spend five minutes today in that specific expression. Not when you feel ready. Today. The flesh doesn't need to feel ready. It needs to yield.

The second action step is to build a weekly worship rhythm that incorporates all seven expressions across the course of a week. You don't have to do all seven every day. But by the end of each week, all seven should have appeared somewhere in your worship life. Assign them to specific days if that helps. Monday, begin with *Barak* and *Yada*. Wednesday, add *Shabach*. Friday, practice *Halal*. During your regular music-based worship time, bring in *Zamar*. After your *Zamar* time, transition into *Tehillah*. And weave *Todah*, which is the lifting of hands in specific thanksgiving, into your daily prayers throughout the week. That rhythm isn't a formula. It's a framework that ensures all seven tools are active in your worship life on a consistent basis. Adjust it to fit your schedule. But make sure all seven are showing up every week.

The third action step is to use one specific expression as a targeted atmospheric weapon over your *metron* this week. Pick one person in your sphere who is under spiritual pressure right now. Someone you've been standing in the gap for. Then choose one of the seven expressions that specifically addresses what they're facing. If they're under the spirit of heaviness, use *Halal* over them. Celebrate God foolishly and specifically over their situation. If they're in a season where they need to hear from God clearly, use *Zamar* as a prophetic tool, playing or singing music before God and then listening for what He wants to say about that person. If the atmosphere over their life feels thick and resistant, use *Shabach* and shout the testimony of God over them by name. Use the tool that matches the need. That's a watchman using praise as a precision weapon rather than a general activity. That's the *Shamar* anointing expressed through worship, guarding the people God has assigned to you through the specific, deliberate use of the seven ancient expressions that God designed to govern the spiritual atmosphere over every territory a watchman has been called to protect.

Activation & Reflection

---

1. Which of the seven Hebrew praise expressions — Yadah, Towdah, Shabach, Halal, Zamar, Barak, or Tehillah — feels most natural to you? Which is most unfamiliar, and why?

____

____

____

____

2. How has your understanding of praise as a spiritual weapon changed or expanded through this chapter?

____

____

____

____

3. Describe a time when breakthrough came through praise rather than petition. What shifted in the atmosphere?

____

____

____

____

4. Which type of praise do you sense God calling you to grow in right now, and why?

____
____
____
____

5. Write a brief declaration using at least three of the Hebrew praise forms as a prophetic act of warfare over a current situation in your life.

____
____
____
____

A Praise Offering

Lord God, I lift every Hebrew expression of praise to You now. I Yadah — I extend my hands in confession of who You are. I Shabach — I shout Your praise with a voice of triumph. I Halal — I celebrate You with joyful abandon. I Zamar — I make melody from the depths of my spirit. I Barak — I kneel before You in reverent blessing. I Towdah — I thank You for what is not yet seen. And I offer my Tehillah — the quiet song of intimacy from a heart that knows You. You are worthy of it all. In Jesus' name, Amen.

CHAPTER 12

Sanctifying the Mind and the Ear Gate

The Battle for the Ear Gate

Romans 10:17 says that faith comes by hearing. Most believers have quoted that verse hundreds of times. But here's what doesn't get said in the same breath: fear comes by hearing too. Discouragement comes by hearing. Doubt comes by hearing. The lie that you're not called, not qualified, not enough, comes by hearing. The ear gate is the primary entry point for everything that shapes what you believe, and that makes it the primary target for the enemy's strategy against every watchman who dares to stand on the wall.

You can't guard your family and your city if your own mind is compromised. You can't stand in the gap for others while the enemy is successfully running his strategy through your own thought life. The *Shamar* anointing over your assigned territory begins with the *Shamar* anointing over your own mind. You can't give out what you don't have. And a watchman whose ear gate is unguarded is a watchman who's being fed lies at the same time they're trying to pray truth.

This is why this chapter matters so much.

The ear gate is exactly what it sounds like. It's the gateway through which sound, words, and information enter your inner world. What goes through that gate doesn't stay neutral. It lands in the soil of your mind and it grows. If what you hear consistently is the Word of God, what grows is faith, clarity, and spiritual authority. If what you hear consistently is the enemy's narrative, what grows is fear, confusion, and the kind of double-mindedness that James 1:7 says disqualifies you from receiving anything from the Lord. The gate determines the harvest. And the watchman who doesn't guard their ear gate will find themselves trying to pray from a compromised inner environment, wondering why their decrees don't carry the weight they should.

Here's something that changes everything about how you understand your own thought life. Not every thought you have came from you. That's not a theological idea. That's a spiritual reality confirmed by 2 Corinthians 10:5, which says to cast down imaginations and every high thing that exalts itself against the knowledge of God. Read that carefully. "Every high thing that exalts itself against the knowledge of God." That means there are thoughts that arrive in your mind whose entire purpose is to contradict what God says about you. They're not your thoughts. They didn't originate from you. They didn't come from God. They came from the enemy. And they came in through the ear gate.

Think about what that means practically. When a thought arrives that says, "You're not really called to this. Your prayers aren't doing anything. God isn't listening. You're too broken to be used," that's not your voice. That's not God's voice. That's a missile. The enemy fires it at your mind and then waits to see what you do with it. If you own it, if you receive it as your own thought and begin to war with it internally, it tightens around you. The more you fight it with more thoughts, the stronger its grip becomes. You can't win a battle of thoughts with more thoughts. You'll exhaust yourself and the lie will still be there, louder than when it started.

This is one of the most common traps that intercessors fall into. They feel a thought that grieves them, something dark, something that contradicts everything they believe about God or about themselves, and they immediately assume they must have produced it. They think, "I can't believe I would think that." And they start fighting themselves. They war internally, condemning themselves for a thought they didn't even generate. They own something that was never theirs to own. And the enemy sits back and watches them exhaust themselves fighting a battle they were never supposed to fight that way.

The three spirits that come against every watchman on the wall, Sanballat's discouragement, Tobiah's slander, and the Ashdodite spirit's confusion, all operate through the ear gate. They don't always show up as external opposition. Sometimes they show up as internal thoughts that feel like your own voice. Sanballat sounds like your own tired, discouraged inner monologue. Tobiah sounds like your own self-doubt. The Ashdodite spirit sounds like your own confusion about your calling. But they're not you. They're missiles fired at your mind through the ear gate. And the moment you recognize them as external attacks rather than internal failures, you gain the upper hand.

The atmosphere around you also feeds through the ear gate in ways you may not have considered. What you listen to when you're not actively choosing shapes what enters your mind passively. The music you leave on in the background. The conversations you allow to stay in your space. The news you consume before you go to sleep. The voices you've given access to through your phone and your social media. All of it is passing through the ear gate. All of it is landing somewhere in the soil of your mind. Demons don't need to get inside you if they can infiltrate your atmosphere. A watchman who prays powerfully in the morning and then spends the rest of the day feeding their ear gate with voices that contradict everything they prayed is building and tearing down at the same time. The net result is very little forward movement.

Think about a woman named Simone, a 36-year-old intercessor who has been standing in the gap for her teenage son for two years. She wakes up early. She prays. She decrees. She builds her case in the courts of heaven with genuine faith and authority. But by midday, she's listening to conversations at work that are full of anxiety and hopelessness about the next generation. By evening, she's scrolling through content that leaves a residue of fear and discouragement in her spirit. By the time she goes to bed, the faith she built in the morning has been significantly eroded by what she allowed through her ear gate for the rest of the day. She's not sinning. She's not being careless on purpose. She just hasn't understood that the ear gate doesn't only matter during prayer time. It matters all day, every day. Because what goes in through that gate is what the enemy has to work with in her thought life. And a compromised ear gate produces a compromised prayer life, no matter how sincere the intentions are.

The *Shamar* watchman who understands the ear gate takes it seriously as a gatekeeping responsibility. You are the gatekeeper of your own mind. No one else can do it for you. God gave you the authority to decide what gets through that gate and what doesn't. And the quality of your intercession, the clarity of your spiritual perception, the weight of your decrees in the courts of heaven, all of it is directly connected to what you've been allowing through the ear gate in the hours and days before you pray.

So what does active gatekeeping look like in practical terms? It starts with an honest audit. Take a full day and pay attention to everything that enters your ear gate. Not just what you deliberately choose to listen to, but what you're passively exposed to. Conversations. Background media. Notifications. The voices you've given consistent access to. At the end of that day, ask yourself one question: did what I heard today build faith or build fear? Did it clarify my assignment or cloud it? Did it draw me toward God's perspective or push me toward the enemy's narrative? You don't have to be perfect in what you allow. But you do need to be honest about what you're currently allowing and what it's producing in your inner world.

Once you've done that audit, make specific decisions. Not vague intentions to "be more careful." Specific decisions. This specific show is out because of the spiritual residue it leaves. This specific conversation pattern is going to change because it consistently feeds discouragement into my ear gate. This specific habit of checking my phone first thing in the morning is being replaced with the Word of God first thing in the morning. Specific. Named. Decided. Because the ear gate doesn't guard itself. You guard it. And you guard it with specific, deliberate choices about what you allow in, not with good intentions that never translate into changed behavior.

The watchman who guards their ear gate is a watchman who shows up to prayer with a clean environment to work from. Their mind isn't already cluttered with the enemy's narrative before they've said a word. Their inner world is ready to receive from heaven because they've been intentional about what they've been feeding it. And when a thought arrives that contradicts what God says, they recognize it immediately for what it is. Not their voice. Not God's voice. A missile. And they know exactly what to do with it.

Shattering the Lie with Verbal Truth

You cannot fight a thought with a thought. This is one of the most important things you'll ever learn about spiritual warfare at the level of the mind. When a lie arrives in your thinking, the instinct is to argue with it internally. To counter it with better reasoning. To analyze where it came from and then debate it in your own head until it goes away. But that strategy doesn't work. It never works. The more you engage a lie internally, the tighter it gets. It feeds on your attention. Every thought you direct at it, even the thought that's trying to refute it, gives it more oxygen. It grows in the space you give it. And by the time you've been fighting it internally for an hour, the only thing filling your mind is the very thought you were trying to get rid of.

The weapon against a lie is not a better thought. The weapon is your voice.

When you speak the Word of God out loud, you're doing something that has two simultaneous effects. First, you're sending truth into the spirit realm as a decree. You're issuing a legal statement that the enemy's suggestion has no authority in the territory of your mind. Second, and this is what most people miss, you're sending that truth back through your own ear gate. The Word you speak goes into your ears. And what goes into the ear gate begins to displace what was already sitting in the mind. The lie can't hold its ground when truth is being fed through the same gate it entered. Faith comes by hearing. So does freedom. So does clarity. So does the shattering of every suggestion the enemy tried to plant in your thinking.

This is the principle behind Romans 10:10, which says that with the mouth, confession is made. Not just with the mind. With the mouth. There's a reason God designed confession as a spoken act. Because what comes out of your mouth goes into your own ears. And what goes into your ears through the Word of God begins to do the work that internal debate never could. It plucks out the lie. Not through argument. Through displacement. The truth crowds out the false thing the same way living water pushes out stagnant water. But it has to be spoken. It has to go through the gate.

Jesus modeled this in the wilderness. When the enemy came at Him with distortion and suggestion, He didn't engage in an internal debate. He didn't sit in silence and try to think His way through the attack. He spoke. "It is written." Three times. Three direct, verbal confessions of specific scripture against specific lies. He out-spoke the enemy. And the enemy left. That's not just a story about Jesus being spiritually superior. That's a pattern. That's the model for how the mind is defended. Not through better thinking. Through spoken truth that enters the ear gate and shatters the power of what the enemy planted there.

Paul understood this when he wrote Ephesians 6:17 about the sword of the Spirit, which is the Word of God. A sword is a weapon you hold in your hand and use actively. It's not something that works while you leave it in the scabbard. You have to draw it. You have to swing it. In the context of the mind and the ear gate, drawing the sword means opening your mouth and speaking the Word out loud. Not thinking about the Word. Not agreeing with the Word internally. Speaking it. Out loud. Into the atmosphere. Through your own ears and into the soil of your mind where the lie is trying to take root.

There's a specific process for using verbal truth as an emergency response when a thought arrives that you recognize as a missile. It has three steps and they need to happen in order. The first step is to recognize. The moment a thought arrives that contradicts what God says about you or your assignment, you name it out loud. Not to the thought. To God. You say, "This thought is not from me and it's not from God. It's a missile from the enemy." That act of naming it does something critical. It removes you from ownership of the thought. You stop fighting yourself and you start identifying the actual source. You're not the problem. The thought is the problem. And naming it that way is the beginning of your counter-attack.

The second step is to find the specific scripture that directly contradicts the specific lie. Not a general scripture. The specific one. If the thought says you're not called, you speak out loud: "I decree that the gifts and calling of God are irrevocable, according to Romans 11:29. My calling is not canceled by this thought. It was established before I was born and it stands right now in the name of Jesus." If the thought says your prayers aren't doing anything, you speak out loud: "I decree that the effective prayer of a righteous person accomplishes much, according to James 5:16. My prayers are not bouncing off the ceiling. They're landing in the courts of heaven and they're producing results I may not see yet. I am righteous through the blood of Jesus Christ and my prayers accomplish much." Specific. Named. Spoken out loud. That's the sword being drawn and swung at a specific target.

The third step is to keep speaking until you feel the shift. This is where most people give up too early. They speak the truth once, feel the same way they did before, and conclude that it didn't work. But the Word doesn't always produce an immediate emotional shift. It produces a spiritual shift first. The lie's grip on the mind loosens before the feeling changes. And the feeling changes after you've been consistent in feeding truth through the ear gate long enough for the displacement to happen. Keep speaking. Keep sending truth through the gate. Don't measure effectiveness by how you feel after one declaration. Measure it by the faithfulness of your speaking over time. Because the more consistently you send the Word through your ear gate, the less room the lie has to breathe.

There's a powerful illustration of how this works that comes from the experience of someone who encountered the enemy's voice early in their walk with God. At sixteen years old, newly saved and full of fire for Jesus, a voice came. Not audible. But clear. A suggestion so dark and so contrary to everything they believed that it stopped them cold. The thought said they wanted to be exalted like Jesus. It was a lie, a dark, accusatory suggestion designed to make them doubt their own heart. And it worked. For weeks, that thought tormented them internally. They fought it with more thoughts. They argued with it in their own mind. They told themselves it wasn't true. But the more they fought it internally, the tighter it got. The more they tried to reason their way out of it, the more it filled their thinking. Until one day they went to a pastor and spoke it out loud. They released the lie verbally. They said what the enemy had been saying to them. And the moment it left their mouth, something broke. The pastor spoke truth back. And when the truth went in through the ear gate, the power of the lie shattered. Not through better thinking. Through speaking the lie out and speaking truth in. That's the mechanism. That's how the ear gate works in both directions. And that's why verbal confession of both the lie you're releasing and the truth you're receiving is the most effective weapon against mental attack.

This has direct implications for the *Shamar* call. A watchman who is under mental attack is a watchman whose effectiveness in intercession is compromised. The enemy knows this. That's why he targets the mind. That's why he fires missiles through the ear gate at the people who are standing in the gap for others. If he can get the watchman fighting their own thoughts, the watchman isn't fighting for the people in their *metron*. The battle for the ear gate is not a personal inconvenience. It's a strategic assault on the effectiveness of your entire assignment. And the way you win it is the same way you win every other battle in the spirit: with the Word of God, spoken out loud, through the very gate the enemy tried to use against you.

There's also a corporate dimension to this that watchmen need to understand. James 5:16 says to confess your faults to one another so that you may be healed. The spoken confession of what you're carrying, whether it's a lie you've been believing, a fear that's been gripping your thinking, a thought pattern that's been compromising your prayer life, doesn't just help you. It breaks something in the spirit when it's spoken in the presence of another believer who can speak truth back into your ear gate. The enemy's power is the power of secrecy. He keeps lies alive by keeping them hidden in the dark of your internal world. When you speak them out in the light, in the presence of a trusted spiritual companion or covering, the power breaks. Not because confession is magic. Because truth spoken into the ear gate of a person who has been carrying a lie is the specific mechanism God designed for shattering that lie's hold. Don't carry mental attacks alone. Speak them out. Let truth come back in. That's the design.

The practical emergency drill for whenever you feel mentally overwhelmed or attacked is this. Stop what you're doing. Don't try to push through it while the attack is at full strength. Stop. Name the thought out loud as a missile. Find the specific scripture that directly contradicts it. Write it down if you need to. Then speak it out loud three times, slowly, letting it go through your ear gate each time. After the third time, say out loud: "I receive this truth into my ear gate right now. I decree that this Word displaces every lie that came in through this gate. My mind is under the blood of Jesus and no weapon formed against it shall prosper." Then go back to what you were doing. If the thought returns, repeat the process. Not with frustration. With the calm authority of a watchman who knows their weapon and knows it works.

The mind is the battlefield. The ear gate is the entry point. And the spoken Word of God is the weapon that wins the battle every time it's used consistently and with faith. A watchman who masters this practice doesn't just protect their own mind. They become someone who can help others do the same. Because when you know how to shatter a lie with verbal truth in your own life, you know exactly how to stand in the gap for someone else who's been hit by the same kind of missile. You can pray for them with precision. You can decree truth over their mind with the authority of someone who has used this weapon personally and knows what it does. That's the *Shamar* anointing operating at its most practical and most powerful level. Guarding the gate. Speaking the truth. Shattering the lie. And staying on the wall.

The Quick-Start Guide

The ear gate is the entry point for both the Word of God and the lie of the enemy. What you allow through that gate shapes what you believe, how you pray, and how effectively you stand in the gap for the people God has assigned to you. A watchman who guards their ear gate guards their entire assignment. A watchman who leaves it unguarded will find themselves fighting internal battles instead of standing in the gap for the people who need them on the wall.

Here's your quick-start guide. Four specific actions. Do them in order this week.

First, do the ear gate audit today. Set a timer for twenty-four hours and pay attention to everything that passes through your ear gate. At the end of that period, write down the three things you heard most consistently that built fear or doubt. Name them specifically. Those three things are your starting point for building a more intentional gatekeeping practice.

Second, identify one recurring negative thought that has been hitting your mind consistently. Not a general category of negative thinking. One specific thought. The one that keeps coming back. The one that the enemy keeps firing at you because he knows it's effective. Write it down on a piece of paper. Then find the specific scripture that directly contradicts it. Write that scripture next to the thought. That pairing is your primary weapon for this season.

Third, speak that scripture out loud every single time that thought attempts to enter your mind. Not sometimes. Every time. You don't have to stop everything you're doing. You speak it wherever you are. In the car. In the kitchen. At your desk. Out loud. The moment the thought arrives, you draw the sword. You speak the truth. You send it through your own ear gate. Do this consistently for twenty-one days and write down in your journal what shifts in the frequency and intensity of that thought over that period.

Fourth, declare your mind a sanctified zone once a day for the next seven days. Every morning before you start your day, speak this out loud: "I declare that my mind is under the blood of Jesus Christ. The ear gate of my soul is guarded by the Word of God. No missile from the enemy has legal access to my thinking today. Every thought that comes is filtered through the truth of what God says about me and my assignment. My mind is clear. My ear gate is clean. I am a *Shamar* watchman standing guard over my own inner world and over the people God has placed in my care." Speak it slowly. Mean it. Let it go through your own ear gate before you go out to face the day.

The *Shamar* anointing over your family and your city starts here. It starts in the mind. It starts at the ear gate. It starts with the daily, specific, faith-filled decision to guard what comes in and to shatter what shouldn't be there with the spoken Word of God. A watchman who wins the battle in their own mind is a watchman who can stand in the gap for everyone else. Guard the gate. Speak the truth. Stay on the wall.

Activation & Reflection

---

1. What voices — media, relationships, fear, culture — have been competing with God's voice through your ear gate? How is that affecting your intercession?

____

____

____

____

2. What does it mean practically to sanctify your ear gate? What specific changes do you need to make in what you listen to daily?

____

____

____

____

3. How has impure information — gossip, fear-based news, cynicism — infiltrated and weakened your prayers?

____

____

____

____

4. Describe a season when your mind was most aligned with God's mind. What habits or disciplines were you practicing then?

____

____

____

____

5. What three specific inputs will you remove from your daily life to create more space for God's voice to speak to you clearly?

____

____

____

____

A Prayer of Mental Sanctification

Lord, I submit my mind and my ear gate to You. I repent of every impure, fearful, and faithless thought I have allowed to take residence. I sanctify my ears — what I listen to, what I watch, what I meditate on — to be a holy channel for Your voice alone. Renew my mind with Your Word. Let my intercession flow from a clean, clear vessel. Guard the gateway of my thoughts, and let only what is true, noble, and pure take root. In Jesus' name, Amen.

CHAPTER 13

Governing Your Atmosphere

There's a moment every watchman eventually faces. You're in a room, a meeting, a family gathering, and something shifts. The atmosphere changes. The conversation gets sharp. Confusion drops in like a cloud. People who were fine ten minutes ago are now irritable, distracted, or pulling away from each other. And if you don't know what you're looking at, you'll spend the next hour trying to fix a natural problem that has a spiritual root.

That's what this chapter is about.

Governing your atmosphere isn't a passive thing. It's not something that happens automatically because you've been praying faithfully. It requires discernment, intentionality, and the willingness to act on what you perceive before the damage is done. The *Shamar* anointing you carry isn't just about standing in the gap in your prayer closet. It's about bringing the authority of that prayer closet into every environment God has assigned to you and actively governing what's allowed to operate there.

Everything you've built in previous chapters, the glory cloud, the washed mind, the legislative decrees, the guarded ear gate, all of it leads to this. Because a watchman who can pray powerfully but can't govern the atmosphere around them is like a guard who knows how to fight but leaves the gate unlocked. The *Shamar* call isn't just about warfare in the secret place. It's about maintaining a clean, holy, glory-filled atmosphere in every space God has put in your care.

Discerning Atmospheric Shifts

One of the most important skills a *Shamar* watchman develops over time is the ability to tell the difference between a natural problem and a spiritual one. Not everything that goes wrong is a demonic attack. People have bad days. Children have behavioral issues. Couples disagree. Fatigue makes people short-tempered. But there's a specific kind of disruption that has a different quality to it, one that comes in too fast, too sharp, and too coordinated to be purely natural. Learning to recognize that quality is what gives you the ability to respond to it correctly before it does lasting damage.

Think about what a demonic cloud actually feels like when it enters a space. It doesn't always announce itself with dramatic manifestations. Most of the time it's subtle. There's a sudden shift in the tone of a conversation that nobody can fully explain. A heaviness settles into a room that wasn't there before. People who were unified start pulling in different directions without knowing why. Children who were calm become agitated. A couple who were fine in the morning are snapping at each other by noon. None of it looks spiritual on the surface. But underneath, there's a specific atmospheric infiltration happening that the natural eye can't see and the untrained spirit can't identify.

The story of a young girl named Peyton is worth thinking about here as an illustration of this principle. Her father noticed that she would suddenly act out in certain environments, not because she was misbehaving, but because she was reacting to something in the atmosphere. She was sensitive to spiritual environments in a way that looked like behavioral trouble on the outside. When he pulled her out of one particular store at the beach, she was fine for the rest of the day. The moment he understood that she was responding to a demonic cloud rather than just misbehaving, everything changed about how he handled it. He stopped trying to correct a behavior problem that wasn't actually a behavior problem. He started governing the atmosphere instead.

That's the shift you need to make as a watchman. You need to develop what could be called a spiritual radar, the ability to perceive what's happening in the unseen realm before it fully manifests in the natural. This isn't about being suspicious of everything or seeing a demon behind every difficulty. It's about being spiritually perceptive enough to recognize when something that looks natural is actually spiritual, and then responding accordingly.

Here's what you're looking for specifically when you're trying to discern whether an atmospheric shift is spiritual or natural. First, look at the speed of it. Natural problems tend to build over time. Spiritual infiltrations tend to hit suddenly. If a room goes from peaceful to chaotic in a way that doesn't match the circumstances, that speed is a signal. Second, look at the coordination of it. When multiple people in the same space are affected in the same way at the same time, that's not coincidence. That's an atmospheric attack hitting a group. Third, look at the irrationality of it. When people can't explain why they're feeling what they're feeling, when the reaction is disproportionate to the situation, that's often a sign that something spiritual is driving what looks like a natural response.

The three spirits you've already learned about, Sanballat's discouragement, Tobiah's slander, and the Ashdodite spirit's confusion, don't just attack individuals. They attack atmospheres. They can infiltrate a room, a meeting, a household, and affect everyone in it simultaneously. The Ashdodite spirit in particular is a master of atmospheric infiltration. It brings a cloud of confusion that settles over a group and makes everyone in it feel foggy, disconnected, and unable to think clearly. When you walk into a meeting and everyone seems off, when the clarity that should be there isn't, when people who are normally sharp seem distracted and scattered, that's often the Ashdodite spirit operating in the atmosphere of that space.

Discernment of this kind develops through two specific practices. The first is consistent time in the presence of God, because the more you know what His atmosphere feels like, the more quickly you recognize when something else is present. You can't identify a counterfeit if you don't know the real thing. The more saturated you are in the glory cloud you've been building through worship and the Word, the more sensitive your spirit becomes to anything that doesn't match it. The second practice is the habit of checking in with your spirit when you enter a new environment. Before you engage with the people in a space, before you jump into the conversation or the meeting, take thirty seconds internally to ask your spirit a simple question: what am I sensing here? You don't need a dramatic prophetic experience. You just need to be present enough to notice what your spirit is already picking up that your mind hasn't processed yet.

When you sense an atmospheric shift, the first thing you do is not panic and not ignore it. You pray quietly in your spirit. Not a loud declaration that draws attention to you. A quiet, internal decree. "I bind the spirit of confusion operating in this atmosphere right now in the name of Jesus. I release the peace of God into this space. Holy Spirit, govern this atmosphere." You don't need to make a scene. You don't need to announce what you're doing. You're a watchman. You do your work from your post, not from a platform. And sometimes the most powerful thing you can do in a room is the thing nobody else in the room can see.

Develop the habit of arriving early to spaces you're responsible for, whether that's your home, your church, or a meeting you're leading, and spending a few minutes praying over the atmosphere before anyone else arrives. Walk through the space. Pray quietly. Declare the atmosphere sanctified. Invite the presence of God. Command anything that doesn't belong to leave in the name of Jesus. You're not performing a ritual. You're doing your job as a *Shamar* watchman. You're governing the atmosphere before the people who need it to be safe arrive. That's the difference between a reactive watchman and a proactive one. The reactive one deals with the infiltration after it's already done damage. The proactive one closes the gate before the enemy gets through.

Here's a specific practice to sharpen your atmospheric discernment this week. Every time you enter a new space, whether it's your home after work, your church building before a service, or a meeting room before a gathering, pause for thirty seconds at the threshold. Don't walk in automatically. Stand at the entrance and check your spirit. Ask yourself three questions silently: what do I feel in this space? Is it consistent with the presence of God or is there something else here? What does my spirit want to do in response? Write down what you notice each time. After a week of doing this consistently, you'll start to see patterns. You'll start to recognize specific spiritual signatures that tell you what kind of atmosphere you've walked into and what kind of response is needed. That's the *Tsaphah* watchman function in practice. You're climbing to the high place and looking out before you engage. You're seeing before you act.

The Art of Territorial Meetings

Every meeting has a spiritual dimension that most people never think about. When two or more people gather, they don't just bring their bodies and their opinions into the room. They bring their atmospheres. They bring whatever spiritual cloud has been forming around their lives, whether it's a cloud of glory or a cloud of something else entirely. And when those atmospheres meet, one of them tends to dominate. The question every watchman needs to be able to answer before a high-stakes meeting is: whose atmosphere is going to govern this space?

Location matters in the spirit more than most believers realize. There's a reason that when you're on your own territory, in your own home, in your church, in a space you've been consistently praying over and governing spiritually, you tend to feel more authority, more clarity, and more confidence. It's not just psychology. It's spiritual. You've been building the atmosphere of that space through your consistent prayer and worship. The glory cloud you carry has been deposited there over time. And when you're operating from within that cloud, you have a home-court advantage that's real in the spirit realm.

The concept of the *metron* applies directly to territorial meetings. Your spiritual authority is strongest in the territory where you've been assigned and where you've built relational and spiritual standing. When you invite someone into your space, you're operating from a position of authority. The atmosphere you've cultivated is the dominant one. But when you go into someone else's territory, especially territory that hasn't been governed spiritually, or worse, territory that's been actively governed by something contrary to the Spirit of God, you're walking into a different dynamic. You're not on home ground. And if you walk in without being spiritually prepared, you can come under the atmosphere of that space rather than governing it.

This is a principle every watchman needs to understand before they walk into sensitive spiritual situations. Deliverance ministry, confrontational conversations, high-stakes negotiations involving spiritual authority, these are situations where the question of territorial advantage is critically important. Doing high-level spiritual work in an unprotected space, or in a space that belongs to someone who isn't aligned with God, can expose you to spiritual contamination that follows you home. That's not fear-based thinking. That's wisdom. The same way a soldier doesn't choose to fight on the enemy's most fortified ground when they can choose better terrain, a watchman doesn't casually walk into spiritually hostile territory without preparation and covering.

There are three principles for navigating territorial meetings with wisdom. The first is to be invited or be sent. Don't go where you haven't been called. If someone needs ministry, prayer, or a difficult conversation, the ideal is that it happens on your territory, in your home or your church, where the atmosphere is already governed and the glory cloud is already present. If you need to go to them, make sure you've been specifically directed by God to do so and that you have the covering of your spiritual authority behind you. Don't go simply because you feel capable. Go because you've been sent.

The second principle is to build your atmosphere before you enter theirs. Before you walk into any high-stakes meeting, especially one that involves spiritual confrontation or deliverance, spend time in prayer and worship to build the cloud you're carrying. Don't go in spiritually flat. Go in carrying the atmosphere of the presence of God. Spend at least fifteen to twenty minutes in genuine worship before you walk through that door. Pray in the Spirit. Decree the presence of God over yourself. Ask the Holy Spirit to go before you and govern the atmosphere of the space you're entering. You're not just preparing yourself emotionally. You're loading the cloud you carry so that when you walk in, the atmosphere you bring is stronger than the one you're walking into.

The third principle is to choose neutral ground when possible for sensitive conversations. When you need to have a spiritually significant conversation with someone and going to their space feels spiritually risky, and inviting them into your home feels premature, a neutral location can be the right choice. A coffee shop, a park, an outdoor space, somewhere that hasn't been governed by either party's spiritual cloud. On neutral ground, the person with the stronger spiritual atmosphere tends to govern the space. And if you've prepared properly, if you've built your cloud before you arrived, that person is you.

Think about a man named Thomas, a 45-year-old pastor who has been asked to meet with a member of his congregation who has been deeply involved in a spiritually oppressive environment. The member wants to meet at their home. Thomas's first instinct is to go, because he wants to serve them. But as he prays about it, he feels a check in his spirit. He asks the member to come to the church instead. Not because he's afraid, but because the church building has been consistently prayed over, anointed, and governed as a sanctuary of the presence of God. The atmosphere of that building works in his favor. When the member arrives and they sit together in that space, something shifts in the member almost immediately. The atmosphere of the church begins to work on them before Thomas has said a word. The cloud that Thomas and his congregation have been building through consistent prayer and worship is doing its job. That's a watchman who understands territorial advantage and uses it wisely.

There's also a specific protocol for when you've been in a spiritually heavy environment and you need to make sure you haven't brought anything back with you. This isn't about fear. It's about hygiene, spiritual hygiene. After any meeting, ministry session, or time spent in a spiritually challenging environment, take time to pray over yourself before you go home. Specifically ask the Holy Spirit to cleanse you of anything that attached itself to your atmosphere during that time. Pray in the Spirit. Declare yourself clean through the blood of Jesus. Ask God to restore the fullness of the glory cloud around your life. Then when you walk through the door of your home, you're not carrying anything in with you that doesn't belong there. You're bringing the cloud of glory, not the residue of someone else's spiritual environment.

Here's your specific action step for territorial meetings. Before your next significant spiritual interaction, whether it's a prayer meeting, a ministry appointment, a difficult conversation with someone in your sphere, or any gathering where you're expected to carry spiritual authority, do this. Twenty minutes before it begins, find a private space and spend that time in worship and prayer. Use at least two of the seven Hebrew expressions of praise to build the cloud you're carrying. Then pray specifically: "Holy Spirit, I ask you to go before me into this meeting. Govern the atmosphere of that space. Let the cloud I carry be the dominant atmosphere in that room. I come as a *Shamar* watchman under the blood of Jesus, and I declare that the presence of God governs this meeting from beginning to end." Then walk in. Don't perform. Don't try to manufacture spiritual authority. Just carry what you've built. The cloud does the work.

Protecting the Home Sanctuary

Your home is supposed to be the most consistently governed spiritual environment in your life. It's the place where your family lives, where your children grow, where your marriage is built, where the most vulnerable people in your sphere spend the most time. If the glory cloud is real anywhere in your life, it should be most consistently present and most consistently protected in your home. But that doesn't happen automatically. It requires intentional, ongoing spiritual governance.

The home is a sanctuary for the glory cloud only when it's treated like one. What you allow inside the walls of your home, both physically and spiritually, determines the atmosphere your family lives in every single day. Not just the obvious things like what you watch or what music plays in the background, though those matter significantly. It's also about who you allow to come in and what they carry with them. It's about what conversations happen in those rooms. It's about whether the Word of God is consistently spoken in that space or whether the dominant voices are everything else. Every one of these things contributes to or erodes the atmosphere you're trying to maintain.

There's a real question that many intercessors face: what do you do when someone comes into your home and leaves something behind? Not physically. Spiritually. You've had people over who seemed fine, but after they left, the atmosphere in your home felt different. The children were more irritable. You and your spouse were more tense with each other. Something that wasn't there before their visit was there after. That's not your imagination. That's a real spiritual dynamic. Demonic atmospheres can be transferred through the presence of people who are carrying them, even when those people aren't aware of it themselves.

This doesn't mean you stop having people in your home. The blessing of God on your home is greater than any spiritual residue a visitor might leave behind. You're not supposed to live in fear of having guests. But you do need to know how to cleanse your home after a visit that left something behind, and you need to be able to recognize when that cleansing is needed. The signs are the same ones you've already learned to recognize as atmospheric infiltration. Sudden tension. Unusual confusion. A heaviness in the air that wasn't there before. When you notice those signs after someone has been in your home, don't just wait for it to lift on its own. Govern the atmosphere.

There's also a specific caution about doing high-level deliverance ministry in your home. When you're engaging in deep spiritual work, casting out spirits, breaking strongholds, dealing with significant demonic oppression, the spiritual activity that's released in that process can leave a residue in the space where it happened. This isn't a reason to never minister in your home. But it is a reason to be thoughtful about it. If you're regularly doing high-level deliverance work, it's worth considering whether a dedicated space outside your home, your church, a prayer room, is more appropriate for that level of ministry. Your home is your family's sanctuary. The spiritual climate of that space affects your children every day. Protect it accordingly.

When you do minister in your home, or when you've had a spiritually heavy visit, the practice of spiritually sweeping your home is essential. This isn't a ritual. It's a *Shamar* function. It's you, as the watchman assigned to that territory, walking through your home and actively governing the atmosphere of every room. Here's exactly how to do it.

Start at the front door. Anoint the doorposts with oil. This is a biblical practice rooted in the Passover, where the blood on the doorposts was a declaration that this household belonged to God and the destroyer had no legal access. Anointing oil in the New Testament context represents the Holy Spirit. When you anoint your doorposts, you're making a spiritual declaration: this home is under the blood of Jesus and the presence of the Holy Spirit governs what comes through this door. As you anoint, speak out loud: "I declare this doorpost anointed in the name of Jesus. Nothing that opposes the presence of God has legal access to this home. This is a sanctuary of the glory cloud."

Then move through each room of your home. In each room, pause and pray specifically. You're not just saying a general prayer over the whole house. You're governing each space individually. In the children's rooms, pray specifically for the protection of their minds and their spirits. Decree that no spirit of confusion, fear, or deception has access to that space. In the living areas, decree that every conversation that happens in this room is governed by the Spirit of God. In your bedroom, declare it a sanctuary of covenant, peace, and the presence of God. As you move through each room, speak out loud. Command any spirit of chaos, confusion, or heaviness to leave in the name of Jesus. You have the authority to do this. This is your assigned territory. This is your post.

After you've gone through every room, stand in the center of your home or in the main gathering space and make a final declaration. Speak it out loud with the authority of a *Shamar* watchman who knows their assignment: "In the name of Jesus Christ, I declare this home a sanctuary of the presence of God. The glory cloud of the Lord fills every room of this house. No weapon formed against this family within these walls shall prosper. This is a house of prayer, a house of peace, a house of the Holy Spirit. The atmosphere of this home is governed by the Word of God and the blood of Jesus. It is clean. It is holy. It is protected. And it will remain so as long as I stand as the watchman God assigned to this territory."

This practice of spiritually sweeping your home shouldn't be a once-a-year event. It should be a regular part of your *Shamar* assignment. Monthly at minimum. After any heavy spiritual activity or challenging visit, do it immediately. After any season of significant conflict in your home, do it as part of the restoration of the atmosphere. Think of it the way you think of physical cleaning. You don't clean your house once and assume it stays clean forever. You maintain it. You keep it. That's the *Shamar* function applied to your home sanctuary. You keep it and you guard it, consistently and proactively.

There's one more dimension of protecting the home sanctuary that often gets overlooked. It's the atmosphere you bring home with you. You've been out in the world all day. You've been in environments that aren't governed by the Spirit of God. You've been in meetings, conversations, traffic, workplaces, all kinds of spaces where the spiritual atmosphere is mixed at best and hostile at worst. And when you walk through your front door, you bring whatever you've been carrying all day into the space your family lives in. That's not a small thing.

Develop a practice of what could be called a threshold prayer. Before you walk into your home at the end of the day, pause at the door. Thirty seconds. Pray quietly: "Holy Spirit, I ask you to cleanse me of anything I've picked up today that doesn't belong in my home. I shake off every spiritual residue from every environment I've been in. I come into this home carrying the glory cloud, not the weight of the world. This home is a sanctuary and I'm walking in as the watchman assigned to protect it." Then walk in. That thirty-second practice is one of the most practical things you can do to maintain the atmosphere of your home sanctuary. Because the most consistent source of atmospheric infiltration in most homes isn't the visitors who come in. It's the family members who come home without thinking about what they're bringing with them.

Your children are watching how you govern the atmosphere of your home. They may not have the language for it yet. But they feel it. They feel the difference between a home where the atmosphere is consistently governed and one where it's left unguarded. They feel the peace of a home where the watchman is at their post. And as they grow, that experience of living in a governed atmosphere becomes part of how they understand what it means to carry the *Shamar* anointing themselves. You're not just protecting them right now. You're modeling for them what it looks like to be a guardian. You're showing them that the atmosphere of a space is something that can be governed, that it doesn't just happen to you, that you have authority over it. That's one of the most powerful things you can pass on to the next generation.

Your Post, Your Practice, Your Atmosphere

Everything in this chapter comes down to one reality: you govern your atmosphere, or your atmosphere governs you. There's no neutral ground. The *Shamar* anointing you carry is most powerful when it's operating actively and intentionally in the spaces God has assigned to you. Discernment without action is just perception. Authority without use is just potential. The watchman who sees what's happening in the atmosphere and then responds with precision and authority is the one who actually changes outcomes for the people in their care.

Here are your action steps for this chapter. There are four of them. Do them this week, in order.

The first action step is to do a full spiritual sweep of your home this week. Set aside one hour. Get anointing oil if you have it, olive oil will do. Start at the front door. Anoint the doorposts. Speak the declaration out loud. Then move through every room, one by one, praying specifically over each space. Command any spirit of chaos, confusion, or heaviness to leave in the name of Jesus. Declare each room a zone of the presence of God. End in the center of your home with the final declaration from this chapter. Write the date in your journal when you've done it. That date is your starting point for making this a regular practice.

The second action step is to begin the threshold prayer practice starting today. Every day this week, before you walk through your front door at the end of the day, pause at the threshold and pray the thirty-second cleansing prayer. Don't skip it because you're tired or in a hurry. The days when you're most tired and most rushed are the days when you're most likely to carry something home that doesn't belong there. Make it a non-negotiable habit. By the end of the week it will feel natural. By the end of the month it will feel essential.

The third action step is to identify the next high-stakes meeting or significant spiritual interaction you have coming up and apply the territorial meeting principles from this chapter. Decide in advance whether it should happen on your territory, neutral ground, or theirs. Build your cloud for twenty minutes before it begins. Pray specifically for the Holy Spirit to govern the atmosphere of that space. After the meeting, take five minutes to pray over yourself before you go home. Write down what you observed about the atmosphere during that meeting and whether your preparation made a difference. That observation becomes part of your ongoing education as a *Shamar* watchman.

The fourth action step is to begin practicing atmospheric discernment daily. Every time you enter a new space this week, pause at the threshold for thirty seconds and check your spirit. Ask the three questions: what do I feel here, is this consistent with the presence of God, and what does my spirit want to do in response? Write down your observations each day. By the end of the week you'll have a record of how your discernment is functioning and which environments in your regular life need more consistent spiritual governance from you.

The *Shamar* anointing over your family and your city is built in the daily, practical, unglamorous work of governing the atmosphere of the spaces God has placed in your care. It's the anointing oil on the doorposts. It's the thirty-second threshold prayer. It's the twenty minutes of cloud-building before a meeting. It's the quiet decree in a room that nobody else heard but that shifted something in the spirit. This is what it looks like to be a guardian. Not just in the prayer room. In every room you've been assigned to keep.

Activation & Reflection

---

1. What atmosphere are you currently creating in your home, workplace, or church through your words, attitudes, and prayers?

____

____

____

____

2. Identify one area of your life where the spiritual atmosphere has been polluted. What has contributed to that, and what will you do to shift it?

____

____

____

____

3. How does your personal prayer altar affect the spiritual climate of your household?

____

____

____

____

4. What decrees or declarations does God want you to regularly speak over your territory to establish and maintain a godly atmosphere?

____

____

____

____

5. Describe what your ideal spiritual atmosphere looks like at home, in your church, and in your city — then write a declaration calling it into existence.

____

____

____

____

An Atmospheric Decree

Father, I take authority over the atmosphere of my home, my church, and my community. I decree that the air is clear of confusion, fear, depression, and division. I release the atmosphere of heaven — peace that passes understanding, joy unspeakable, and the glory of Your manifest presence. I am a thermostat, not a thermometer — I set the spiritual temperature, I do not merely read it. Let heaven's atmosphere be established in every space I steward. In Jesus' name, Amen.

CHAPTER 14

The Principle of Prevenient Grace

There's a peace that's available to every intercessor that most of them never fully walk in. It's not the peace of having everything figured out. It's not the peace that comes from seeing every prayer answered exactly the way you hoped. It's something deeper than that. It's the peace of knowing that because you said yes to God, because you came into alignment with Christ and took your place as a watchman over your family, something has already been legally established in heaven on behalf of the people you love. Something is already working on their behalf before they ever feel it, before they ever respond to it, before they ever even know it's there. That's prevenient grace. And understanding it changes everything about how you carry your assignment.

Most intercessors are carrying more fear than they need to. They're praying hard, staying faithful, standing in the gap, and yet somewhere underneath all of that faithfulness is a quiet terror. What if my child never comes home? What if my spouse never turns around? What if I pray my whole life and they still don't make it? That fear is real. It's understandable. But it's based on a misunderstanding of what your covenant with God actually does for the people connected to you.

This chapter is going to give you something you can stand on. Not a feeling. A legal reality.

Covenant Coverage for the Household

When you came into alignment with Jesus Christ, something happened that went beyond your own salvation. Your decision to follow Him didn't just change your eternal destination. It activated a covenant that carries legal implications for every person connected to you by blood and by household. That covenant creates what theologians call prevenient grace, a grace that goes before, that precedes, that covers people who haven't yet responded to God themselves but who are connected to someone who has.

The word "prevenient" simply means "coming before." Prevenient grace is God's grace that goes ahead of a person, working on them before they're even aware of it, drawing them, hedging them in, keeping them from going so far that they can't come back. It's the grace that keeps the prodigal son from dying in the pigpen. It's the grace that makes the far country eventually feel unbearable. It's the grace that creates the conditions for a person to "come to themselves," as Jesus described it in Luke 15, even when they've been running hard in the wrong direction.

And here's what makes this so significant for the *Shamar* watchman: that grace is activated over your household by your covenant with God.

The promise in Acts 16:31 isn't just a nice sentiment. "Believe in the Lord Jesus Christ and you will be saved, you and your household." That's a covenant statement. It's a legal declaration that your faith creates a covering over the people in your house. Not that they're automatically saved without choosing it themselves. God never overrides the will of a person. But it means that the grace of God is actively working on them in a way it wouldn't be if there were no covenant believer in the family. They're not just randomly floating through life hoping they somehow find their way to God. They're being hedged in by a grace that's working specifically because you are in covenant with the One who holds all grace.

Think about what that actually means for the person you're carrying the most burden for right now. The child who walked away. The parent who's never received Jesus. The sibling who's been living far from God for years. They may look free. They may look like they're doing whatever they want with no spiritual interference. But from heaven's perspective, they're not free. They're hedged in. The grace of God is surrounding them, working on them, setting up circumstances, orchestrating encounters, creating moments of conviction, keeping doors closed that would take them somewhere they can't come back from. They're being kept until they're ready to say yes. And your covenant with God is the legal basis for that keeping.

This is not a passive thing on your part. You still pray. You still stand in the gap. You still issue decrees. But you do it from a completely different posture when you understand prevenient grace. You're not praying from a place of terror, hoping God notices and does something. You're praying from a place of legal standing, reminding heaven of a covenant that's already in effect, reinforcing a hedge that's already up, and asking God to intensify the work of grace that's already operating in the life of your loved one.

It's worth being specific about what this grace actually does in the life of an unsaved person who has a covenant believer praying for them. First, it limits the damage the enemy can do. There's a boundary around that person that the enemy can't cross without permission, because the watchman's prayers are creating a legal barrier. The enemy can still tempt them. He can still put pressure on them. But he can't destroy them outright, because there's a covenant covering over their life that he has to contend with. Second, the grace creates a longing. It builds a hunger in them for something more, even when they can't name what that something is. People who have covenant intercessors praying for them often describe, after they come to God, a sense that something was always drawing them. A restlessness they couldn't explain. A knowing that there was more. That's prevenient grace doing its work. Third, it sets up divine appointments. God orchestrates encounters, conversations, and circumstances specifically designed to create an opening for that person to respond to Him. The right person shows up at the right time. A song plays at a moment of vulnerability. A crisis creates a crack in the wall of resistance. None of it is random. It's the strategic work of grace that's been activated by the prayers of a watchman.

Think about a woman named Renata, a 38-year-old who has been walking with God for twelve years. She has two adult siblings who have never given their lives to Christ. One of them is in a lifestyle that looks, from the outside, like it's going in a very bad direction. Renata prays for them faithfully, but she's been carrying a weight of fear that they might not make it. She's been praying from a place of desperation rather than from a place of covenant standing. When someone teaches her about prevenient grace, something shifts in her. She stops praying as if God hasn't noticed her siblings. She starts praying as a covenant believer who knows that the grace of God is already surrounding them, already working on them, already setting up the conditions for their return. She doesn't stop praying. She actually prays more specifically. But she stops being afraid. And that shift in her posture changes the quality and the authority of everything she brings before God on their behalf.

The legal basis for prevenient grace over your household isn't your perfection. It's your covenant. You don't have to be a perfect spouse, a perfect parent, or a perfect believer for the covering to be in effect. What activates it is your alignment with Christ. Your decision to follow Him. Your willingness to stand in the gap. The moment you said yes to Jesus, the covenant went into effect. And that covenant covers the people connected to you in ways that are still unfolding, still working, still pressing them toward the day when they will say yes themselves.

There's also something important to understand about the single believer in a household. You don't need two covenant believers for this covering to work. The Bible addresses this directly. In 1 Corinthians 7:14, Paul says that the unbelieving spouse is sanctified through the believing one. That word "sanctified" doesn't mean saved. It means set apart, covered, brought under the influence of something holy. The believing spouse creates a spiritual environment that affects the entire household, including the one who hasn't yet responded to God. If you're the only believer in your home, your covenant with God is still sufficient to activate prevenient grace over everyone under that roof. The covering doesn't require two people. It requires one person who is genuinely in covenant with the One who holds all authority in heaven and on earth.

This is also why the *Shamar* anointing over your family is not just about prayer in the conventional sense. It's about your life. The way you carry yourself. The way you serve the people in your home. The way you love your spouse even when they're difficult. The way you respond to your children with grace instead of frustration. The way you maintain your integrity in the small, daily moments that nobody outside the house ever sees. All of that is part of how the covering operates. It's not just what you decree in your prayer closet. It's what you model in your kitchen. The unbelieving spouse, according to 1 Corinthians 7, is won not primarily through argument but through witnessing Christ in the life of the believing partner. Your humility. Your consistency. Your willingness to serve without demanding recognition. That's the prevenient grace made visible. That's the covering becoming tangible in a way that the people in your home can actually see and feel.

So here's what you need to do specifically with this truth. Stop praying for your unsaved family members from a place of fear and start praying from a place of covenant standing. The next time you bring them before God, begin not with desperation but with declaration. Say out loud: "Father, I come before your court right now as a covenant believer. I stand on Acts 16:31 as my legal ground. My household is under the covering of prevenient grace because I am in covenant with you. I thank you that your grace is already working on every unsaved person connected to me. I thank you that they are hedged in, that the enemy cannot destroy them, and that you are orchestrating the conditions for their return. I reinforce that hedge right now through my prayers. I ask you to intensify the work of grace in their lives. Set up the divine appointments. Create the moments of conviction. Make the far country unbearable and the Father's house irresistible." That's not a desperate prayer. That's a covenant watchman reinforcing what's already legally in effect.

You don't have to live in fear for your unsaved loved ones. That's not the posture of a *Shamar* watchman who understands prevenient grace. You pray with urgency, yes. You stay at your post, absolutely. But you stand in the gap from a place of settled confidence that the grace of God is already doing what you can't do. It's already working in ways you can't see. It's already surrounding the people you love with a covering that's rooted in your covenant with the most powerful being in the universe. That's not small. That's the legal reality of what your yes to God has established. Stand on it.

The Power of the Vow

There's a dimension of the watchman's assignment that goes beyond regular intercession. It's the dimension of the vow. The specific, intentional agreement made with God that secures something in the spirit realm and creates a legal record in the courts of heaven that outlasts a single prayer session. It outlasts a season. In some cases, it outlasts a lifetime.

David made vows to God. Solomon inherited the benefit of those vows even when his own behavior didn't deserve it. In 1 Kings 11:12, after Solomon had turned away from God and God declared that the kingdom would be torn from him, God said, "Nevertheless I will not do it in your days, for the sake of your father David." David was dead. But the vow he had made, the altar he had built, the covenant he had established with God through a life of worship and sacrifice, was still legally active in the courts of heaven. It was protecting his son from the full consequences of his own choices. The altar David built didn't disappear when David died. It kept standing. And it kept covering.

That's the power of a vow. It creates a spiritual structure that extends beyond the moment you make it. It builds something in the spirit that continues to function after you're gone. When you make a specific vow to God, when you say, "Lord, I commit to this specific act of obedience or sacrifice, and I'm asking you to respond by covering this specific person or situation," you're not just making a prayer request. You're building an altar. And altars in the spirit realm have legal standing. They create a claim on heaven's resources that the courts of heaven recognize and honor.

Think about what this means for your bloodline. The vows you make today, the altars you build through your sacrificial giving, your consistent intercession, your faithful service to God's purposes, these things don't just affect your immediate situation. They create a spiritual inheritance for the people who come after you. Your children will benefit from the altars you build today. Your grandchildren will live under a covering that your vows established before they were born. You're not just praying for the people in front of you. You're shaping the spiritual environment of your entire bloodline for generations to come.

This is one of the most underestimated aspects of the *Shamar* call. Most watchmen think in terms of the immediate. They're praying for the person in front of them, the situation they can see, the need that's pressing right now. And that's right and necessary. But the full scope of the watchman's assignment includes the long view. It includes building spiritual structures that will protect and guide people who aren't born yet. It includes making vows that create a legal covering over your bloodline that the enemy will have to contend with for generations.

A vow is different from a regular prayer in a specific way. A prayer is a conversation. A vow is a contract. When you make a vow to God, you're entering into a binding spiritual agreement. You're saying, "I will do this specific thing, and in response, I'm asking you to do this specific thing." God takes vows seriously. Ecclesiastes 5:4-5 says, "When you make a vow to God, do not delay to fulfill it. He has no pleasure in fools. Fulfill your vow." That's not a warning to discourage you from making vows. It's a confirmation that vows carry real weight in the spirit. They're not casual. They're binding. And when you fulfill them, they create a legal record of faithfulness that becomes part of your case in the courts of heaven.

There's also a specific principle about activated altars that every watchman needs to understand. The story of Jesus feeding the five thousand isn't just a miracle story. It's a lesson in how kingdom principles work. Jesus saw what was coming. He knew the disciples were about to face a storm on the water that was designed to kill them. And instead of just telling them to pray, He activated a principle. He put them in the position of givers. He made them the ones who served the multitude. He made them build an altar of generosity and compassion before the crisis arrived. And when the storm came, the altar they had built created a legal claim on heaven's protection. They could have prayed in that boat, but the prayer alone wouldn't have been enough in that moment. What saved them was the principle they had already activated. The altar was already standing. And it held.

That's the lesson for the watchman who wants to make long-term spiritual investments in their family's future. You don't just pray. You build altars. You make vows. You activate kingdom principles through sacrificial giving, through consecrated prayer, through specific acts of obedience that create a legal record in the courts of heaven. And those altars keep standing long after the moment of their building. They keep covering. They keep protecting. They keep creating the conditions for God to move on behalf of the people you've built them for.

What does a vow look like in practical terms? It's specific. It's personal. It's connected to something you're genuinely willing to commit to. A vow that costs you nothing isn't really a vow. It's a wish. A vow has weight because it involves sacrifice, because it involves you putting something on the altar. Here are some examples of what this can look like for a *Shamar* watchman interceding for their family's future.

A vow of consecrated prayer. You commit to God that you will pray specifically for your bloodline, by name, for a set period of time every day for a defined season. Not a vague intention to pray more. A specific commitment. "God, I vow to you that I will pray for the salvation of my bloodline for thirty minutes every morning for the next year. I'm building this altar of intercession over my family, and I'm asking you to honor it with the grace of salvation for every person in my bloodline." That's a vow. It's specific. It has a defined commitment. And it creates a legal structure in the spirit that God honors.

A vow of sacrificial giving. You commit to give a specific amount or a specific portion of what you have to God's purposes, specifically consecrated to the salvation and destiny of your family. This connects directly to the principle of Psalm 41, which you've already learned. The person who considers the poor and gives sacrificially builds a legal hedge around themselves and their household. When you give specifically as an act of faith for your bloodline, you're activating the principle of generosity as a covenant claim on God's faithfulness toward your family.

A vow of lifestyle consecration. You commit to a specific area of obedience that you've been holding back in. You bring it to God and say, "I'm giving you this area of my life fully. I'm consecrating it to you. And I'm asking you to honor this act of obedience with a specific breakthrough for my family." That kind of vow, rooted in genuine surrender and specific obedience, creates a powerful legal record in the courts of heaven.

Whatever form the vow takes, the key is that it's specific, it's sincere, it costs you something, and you keep it. Because a vow that isn't kept doesn't just fail to build the altar. It actually works against you. Ecclesiastes 5:5 says it's better not to vow than to vow and not fulfill it. So don't make a vow you can't keep. Make one that stretches you but that you're genuinely committed to. And then keep it. Because every day you keep it, you're adding another stone to the altar. You're reinforcing the legal structure in the spirit. You're building something that will still be standing long after you're gone, covering the people in your bloodline who will come after you.

There's also something deeply important about the vows you make over your bloodline that connects to the *Shamar* anointing at its fullest expression. You're not just a watchman for the people alive right now in your family. You're a watchman for the generations. The spiritual structures you build through your vows and your altars are part of the inheritance you leave. Just as David's vows created a covering that protected Solomon even in his failure, your vows can create a covering that protects your children and your grandchildren in their most vulnerable moments. You're building something that outlasts you. That's the long view of the *Shamar* call. That's the watchman who doesn't just guard today's gate but builds walls that will stand for the next generation.

Here's your specific action step for this section. Sit down this week with a blank piece of paper and write the names of the people in your bloodline who aren't yet walking with God. Write every name. Don't filter it. Don't limit it to the ones you think are close. Write them all. Then pray over that list and ask God to show you one specific vow He's calling you to make on their behalf. One specific, concrete commitment that you're genuinely able to keep. Write it down as a formal statement. "God, I vow to you that I will \[specific commitment\] for \[specific time period\], and I'm asking you to honor this altar with the grace of salvation and destiny for the people on this list." Speak it out loud. Date it. Keep it in a place where you'll see it regularly. And then keep the vow. Every day you keep it, the altar grows stronger. Every day you keep it, the covering over your bloodline becomes more established in the courts of heaven. You're not just praying for your family. You're building something that will outlast you and protect them long after you're gone.

Putting It Into Practice

Prevenient grace is the legal result of your covenant with God. The moment you came into alignment with Christ, your family came under a covering that's already working, already active, already surrounding the people you love with a grace that's pressing them toward salvation. You don't have to earn that covering. You don't have to be perfect to maintain it. You simply have to stay in your covenant, stay at your post, and pray from the place of legal standing that your yes to God established.

The power of the vow extends that covering further and deeper. The altars you build through your specific commitments to God create legal structures in the courts of heaven that protect your bloodline for generations. God is a keeper of covenants. He honored David's altar long after David was gone. He will honor yours.

Here are your action steps. There are three of them. Do all three this week.

The first action step is to make your list. Get a piece of paper right now and write the names of every unsaved person in your family and your household. Every name. Don't skip anyone because you think they're too far gone or because you've given up hope. Write them all. Then, next to each name, write this declaration: "Covered by prevenient grace through my covenant with God." Speak each name out loud and speak that declaration over each one. You're not wishing. You're declaring a legal reality that your covenant established. Do this as an act of faith, not of feeling. The feeling will follow the declaration. Keep that list somewhere you'll see it daily.

The second action step is to shift your prayer posture starting today. The next time you pray for any unsaved person on your list, begin by thanking God for the prevenient grace that's already surrounding them. Not asking Him to start working. Thanking Him for the work that's already in progress. Say specifically: "Father, I thank you that your grace is already surrounding \[name\]. I thank you that they are hedged in and that the enemy cannot destroy what you are drawing toward yourself. I reinforce this hedge right now through my prayer. Intensify the work of your grace in their life today." That shift from petition to thanksgiving is a shift in legal posture. You're no longer asking God to start. You're reinforcing what He's already doing.

The third action step is to make one specific vow this week. Just one. Follow the process from the second section of this chapter. Pray and ask God what He's calling you to commit to on behalf of your bloodline. Write it down as a formal statement. Speak it out loud before God. Date it. And begin keeping it today. The altar starts with the first stone. Place it.

The *Shamar* anointing over your family isn't just about what you do in prayer. It's about the legal reality of what your covenant with God has already established. You're not guarding an unprotected family and hoping for the best. You're reinforcing a covering that heaven has already put in place. Stand on that. Pray from that. Build your altars from that place. And trust the God who is faithful to complete what He started, in your life and in the lives of every person your covenant covers.

Activation & Reflection

---

1. How does the concept of prevenient grace — God's grace that goes before and prepares — change the way you pray for unbelievers or hardened hearts?

____
____
____
____

2. Can you identify moments in your own life where prevenient grace was working before you even recognized God's hand?

____
____
____
____

3. How does knowing that God is already at work in the people you pray for free you from anxiety-based or striving intercession?

____
____
____
____

4. Who in your life is currently in a prevenient grace season — unaware of God's pursuit? How does this knowledge fuel your prayers for them?

____
____
____
____

5. How can you position yourself as a co-laborer with prevenient grace — cooperating with what God is already doing rather than trying to force outcomes?

____
____
____
____

A Prayer Cooperating with Grace

Father of mercy, I thank You that Your grace goes before every person I intercede for. You are already at work in hearts I cannot reach — softening, drawing, preparing the soil. I align my prayers with Your prevenient grace today. I release control and join the work You are already doing. Remove every obstacle the enemy has placed in the path of those You are calling. Let every seed of intercession I have planted bear fruit in Your perfect timing. In Jesus' name, Amen.

CHAPTER 15

Sovereignty and the Mercy of Judgment

Understanding the Mercy in the Storm

There's a story in Scripture that most people read and walk away confused. First Chronicles 21 says Satan rose up against Israel and moved David to number the people. But then you go to Second Samuel 24 and read the same event, and it says God moved David to number the people. Same event. Two different accounts. One says Satan. One says God. And if you don't understand what God was actually doing in that moment, you'll spend the rest of your life misreading how He works in the hard seasons of your life and the lives of the people you're standing in the gap for.

David's heart had already turned. Not suddenly. Gradually. Quietly. The way hearts always drift. And God, who loved David deeply, saw it. He saw where that drift was taking him. He saw the eternal destination of a man whose heart was moving away from the source of his life. And so God, in an act that looks terrifying on the surface but is actually the most loving thing He could have done, allowed David to do the very thing that would expose what was already in his heart. He let David number the people. He let the deception run its course. And when the consequences came, David fell on his face before God. He repented. He threw himself at the mercy of the One he had drifted from. And that act of repentance, that breaking, that dismantling of the pride that had been quietly building, saved his soul.

That's mercy. It doesn't always look like mercy. But it is.

This is one of the most sobering and most liberating truths a *Shamar* watchman can carry. God cares more about your eternal destination than your current comfort. He cares more about the soul of the person you're interceding for than about their immediate circumstances staying pleasant. When He allows a person to walk into the consequences of what's in their heart, when He lets the deception run until the crash comes, He's not being cruel. He's being a Father who knows that the crash is the only thing that will bring His child home before it's too late.

Think about what this means for the people in your *metron* who seem to be in a season of complete collapse. The person whose life is falling apart in a way that looks like God has abandoned them. The believer who made choices that led them somewhere dark and now they're living in the rubble of those choices. The prodigal who went so far that you can barely recognize them anymore. From the outside, it looks like judgment. From heaven's perspective, it might be the most merciful thing God could do for that soul. He's tearing down brick by brick everything that was built on a foundation that wasn't Him. Not to destroy them. To save them. To strip away every false thing until all that's left is the one thing they actually need.

The Bible puts it plainly in 1 Corinthians 5:5. Paul speaks of handing someone over to Satan for the destruction of the flesh, but the salvation of the spirit. That's a sentence that should stop you cold. God can use the enemy's own hand to accomplish His redemptive purposes. Not because He approves of the destruction, but because He's sovereign over all of it. Everything in heaven, on earth, and under the earth is subject to Him. He can command a demon the same way He commands an angel. He's not limited by what looks like chaos to us. He's working in it, through it, and despite it to bring His children home.

The deceiver and the deceived are judged by the same measure. That's another piece of this truth that's easy to miss. When Abraham told Sarah to say she was his sister, the king who took her into his household was deceived. He didn't know she was Abraham's wife. He acted in ignorance. And yet God came to him in a dream and said, "If you touch her, you will die." The charge against the deceived king was the same weight as the charge against the one who deceived. Why? Because whatever is in the heart of those who can be deceived is of equal measure against God as the deception itself. The heart that's vulnerable to deception is already carrying something that doesn't belong there. And God's mercy will expose it, even when the exposure looks like judgment.

This isn't about justice. That's the critical distinction. When God allows someone to go through a wreck, when He permits the consequences of a drifting heart to fully manifest, He's not balancing a cosmic ledger. He's reaching for a soul. He's using the only thing that will break through the armor of a heart that's been slowly hardening without knowing it. The wreck is designed to bring them back. Every bit of it. The severity of the mercy is proportional to the depth of the drift. The further someone has gone, the more dramatic the intervention sometimes has to be. Not because God is harsh. Because He's thorough. He won't lose a soul He loves without exhausting every available means to bring them home.

As a *Shamar* watchman, this truth changes how you pray for people in collapse. You stop praying for God to restore what they had. You start praying for God's mercy to do its complete work. You stop asking Him to make the pain stop. You start asking Him to make the pain productive. You stop interceding for the circumstances to improve and you start interceding for the soul to be saved. That's not cold or unfeeling. That's the most loving prayer you can pray for someone in a wreck. Because God doesn't care about right now. He cares about eternity. And a watchman who prays with that perspective is praying from the same heart God has for the people they love.

There's a specific practice to carry this truth into your intercession. The next time you're standing in the gap for someone whose life appears to be in collapse, before you pray for restoration, pray this first: "God, let your mercy do its complete work. Don't let them come out of this the same way they went in. Let every false thing come down. Let every drift be exposed. Let the wreck accomplish what it was sent to accomplish. And bring them home." That prayer is the prayer of a watchman who trusts the sovereignty of God even when it looks like everything is falling apart. It's the prayer that aligns your intercession with what heaven is actually doing rather than asking God to stop what He's in the middle of completing.

The things that are permanent can't be changed. Jesus is coming back. The final judgment is real. The books of heaven are open. These are not negotiable. But the circumstances of a person's life, the path they're currently on, the heart condition that's driving them toward destruction, those are not permanent. They can change through the power of prayer. They can change through the mercy of a God who is willing to use even the storm to bring His children home. Moses stood before God and pleaded for Israel when God said He would destroy them. And God relented. That wasn't luck. That was an intercessor who understood that everything dealing in the earth can be changed through the power of prayer, except what God has already declared permanent. The storm can change. The heart can change. The destination can change. But only if someone is standing in the gap, praying not for comfort but for completion, not for ease but for eternity.

That's the mercy in the storm. And a watchman who understands it doesn't run from the hard seasons in the lives of the people they're assigned to guard. They lean in. They pray harder. They stand firmer. Because they know that the storm isn't the end of the story. It's the mercy of God working to write a better one.

Ambassadors vs. Rebels

There's a difference between going and being sent. It sounds simple. But it's the difference between walking in the full backing of heaven and walking into a fight you were never equipped to win alone. The sons of Sceva thought they could go. They saw what Paul was doing. They heard the name of Jesus being used with power. And they walked up to a man with an evil spirit and said, "We command you in the name of Jesus whom Paul preaches." The demon looked at them and said, "Jesus I know, and Paul I know, but who are you?" And then it attacked them. They ran out of that house naked and wounded.

They went. They weren't sent.

An ambassador doesn't move on their own initiative. An ambassador moves with the full authority and resources of the government that sent them. When a diplomat walks into a foreign nation, they don't go as a private citizen hoping things go well. They go representing the full weight of their home country. The authority they carry isn't personal. It's positional. It flows from the one who sent them. And that distinction matters enormously in the spirit realm, because demons don't respond to personal confidence. They respond to delegated authority. They respond to the legal backing of a sender whose jurisdiction they have to recognize.

This is why accountability isn't a restriction on the *Shamar* call. It's the source of its power.

When you're properly aligned with Christ and properly covered by your spiritual authority, when you move into an assignment with the blessing of the one God has placed over your life, you don't go alone. Their grace goes with you. Their angels extend to cover your territory. The battles you face in that assignment have a higher authority engaged on your behalf. But when you go without being sent, when you push into spiritual warfare in a region where you have no assignment and no covering, you expose yourself to a backlash that the enemy has every legal right to bring against you. He's not attacking you because he's more powerful. He's attacking you because you stepped into his territory without authorization. And the spirit world knows the difference.

There's a real and sobering illustration of this principle in the story of a young minister who went to Atlanta in his twenties, burning with zeal, and began commanding principalities to fall over the city. He wasn't malicious. He was passionate. He loved God. But he had no assignment there. No covering in that region. No invitation from the spiritual authority of that land. He was going, not being sent. And on his way home, a car hit his vehicle head-on at high speed. The collision broke his ribs. His vehicle was destroyed. What he understood afterward was that the spirit he had confronted in Atlanta followed him back to his own region to retaliate. Demons have assignments, not just geographical locations. They're rebellious by nature. And when you walk into their territory without authorization, they don't just let it go. They come after you where you're most vulnerable.

That's not a story meant to produce fear. It's a story meant to produce wisdom. The watchman who understands the principle of being sent doesn't shrink from spiritual warfare. They become more precise about it. They ask the right questions before they move. Am I properly aligned with Christ right now? Is there anything between me and God that needs to be addressed before I step into this? Am I properly covered? Does the spiritual authority in my life know what I'm doing and have they released me to do it? Am I invited or am I being sent? Is there someone with authority in this territory who has asked me to come and pray?

All three questions need a clear yes before you move into high-level confrontation.

Being invited means someone with authority in that region has specifically asked you to come and pray. Being sent means God has directed you to go and your spiritual covering has confirmed it. Both matter. If you're invited but not sent, you might be going for the wrong reasons. If you feel sent but no one in authority over you has confirmed it, slow down. God works through order. He doesn't bypass the structure He designed. And when you honor that structure, the grace of your covering goes with you. When you bypass it, you go alone. And a watchman who goes alone into high-level spiritual warfare is a watchman who's one confrontation away from being overwhelmed.

There's also a dimension of divine timing that every watchman must learn to honor. Not just where you go, but when. There are seasons when God is preparing something in a territory and the timing of your intercession matters enormously. Moving before the appointed time can actually disrupt what God is setting up. Moving after the window closes means the moment has passed. The watchman who is properly aligned with their covering, who is consistently in the *Tsaphah* posture of watching from the tower and waiting for God to speak, will know the timing. They won't move out of zeal. They'll move out of assignment. And the difference in the spiritual results will be dramatic.

The rebel moves when they feel ready. The ambassador moves when they're sent. The rebel fights with their own strength. The ambassador fights with the full backing of the government they represent. The rebel faces the enemy alone. The ambassador faces the enemy with heaven's resources behind them. And when the battle is over, the rebel comes home wounded and confused about what went wrong. The ambassador comes home carrying the fruit of a victory that was never really theirs to win in the first place. It was always heaven's victory. They were just the one who was sent to stand in the gap and enforce it.

Here's what you need to do specifically to walk in the full authority of an ambassador rather than the exposure of a rebel. First, before any significant act of spiritual warfare or any assignment that takes you outside your established *metron*, bring it to your spiritual covering. Not as a formality. As a genuine act of submission. Tell them what you're sensing. Ask them to pray over it. Ask them to confirm or redirect. If they confirm it, receive their blessing and go knowing their grace goes with you. If they redirect, trust that God is protecting you from something you can't fully see. Second, when you're in a territory or a situation where you feel spiritual opposition that's bigger than your personal authority, don't try to push through it alone. Reach back to your covering. Ask them to pray. Let their higher authority engage in the battle on your behalf. That's not weakness. That's kingdom wisdom. It's the same thing Peter did when Jesus told him that Satan had demanded a trial against him. Jesus said, "I have prayed for you." Peter didn't fight that battle alone. He had someone of higher authority standing in the gap for him. That's the covering principle operating exactly as God designed it.

Third, guard against the spirit of zeal that looks like faith but operates like rebellion. Zeal is good. Passion for God is good. But zeal without submission is dangerous. The most zealous intercessors are often the most vulnerable to this trap because they genuinely love God and genuinely want to see things shift. But love for God doesn't override the need for order. It actually deepens it. Because the person who truly loves God also loves what God loves. And God loves the order He designed. He loves the structure of covering and sending. He loves the watchman who moves in alignment, not just in passion. When your zeal is submitted to your covering, it becomes a force the enemy can't stand against. When it's unsubmitted, it becomes an open door.

A lot of people feel like the requirement to be sent is a restriction. God calls it protection. There are places you shouldn't go even if you want to go. There are battles you shouldn't engage even if you feel capable of engaging them. The boundary of your assignment isn't a limitation of your calling. It's the shape of your authority. And a watchman who stays within the shape of their authority, who moves only when sent and only in alignment with their covering, carries a weight in the spirit that a rebel can never access. Because the weight isn't theirs. It belongs to the One who sent them. And the One who sent them is the most powerful force in the universe.

The Final Call to the Wall

We are closer to the return of Jesus Christ than we have ever been. That's not a statement meant to create anxiety. It's a statement meant to create urgency. The East Gate is the gate Nehemiah's roadmap points toward, the gate through which the King will return. And the gap between where we are right now and that moment is narrowing every single day. The enemy knows it. That's why the pressure is intensifying. That's why the attacks on families, on churches, on intercessors are heavier than they've ever been. He's working overtime because he knows his time is short.

And God is looking for people who will stand in the gap.

Ezekiel 22:30 says He looked for a man who would stand in the hedge and found none. That verse should shake every person who carries the *Shamar* anointing. We are approaching the coming of Christ and we've lost our desire to pray. That's the danger. Not just that the world is getting darker. The danger is that the people who are supposed to be standing in the gap are distracted, discouraged, and disconnected from the urgency of the hour. A watchman without urgency is just a person standing on a wall. The urgency of the East Gate is what turns a prayer life into a kingdom assignment.

Nehemiah never came off the wall. Three spirits came at him. Sanballat brought discouragement. Tobiah brought slander. The Ashdodites brought confusion. All three at the same time. And the Bible says he built with one hand and fought with the other. He never stopped building. He never came down. Because he understood that there were too many souls on the line to let the enemy's strategy succeed. There were people inside the walls who needed those walls to go up. There were people whose safety, whose future, whose destiny depended on one man staying at his post when everything in the natural was screaming at him to quit.

That's your assignment right now.

Every person in your *metron* is somewhere in the Nehemiah cycle. Some of them are still at the Sheep Gate, not yet saved, being drawn by the prevenient grace that your covenant with God has activated over your household. Some of them are stuck between the Valley Gate and the Dung Gate, going around the same mountain, unable to release what the valley was supposed to remove. Some of them are standing right at the edge of the Water Gate, right on the threshold of their divine purpose, being held back by the spirit of fear that the enemy sends to every person who's about to step into what God wrote about them before they were born. Every single one of them needs a watchman who won't come down.

Standing in the gap means more than showing up to pray when you feel like it. It means positioning yourself between heaven and earth so that the things that are supposed to happen will happen and the things that are not supposed to happen will not happen. It means praying people through the cycle even when you can't see any movement. It means decreeing over your city even when the atmosphere feels resistant. It means staying at your post through the discouragement of Sanballat, through the slander of Tobiah, through the confusion of the Ashdodite spirit, because you understand that the wall isn't finished yet and the people inside it still need you there.

Think about what happens when a watchman leaves their post. The enemy doesn't announce himself. He moves quietly. Division slips into a church through a small disagreement that should have been prayed through before it became a public argument. Confusion settles over a family that should have had a watchman standing guard over the atmosphere of that home. A young person makes a decision that changes the trajectory of their life, and nobody was praying them through the gate they were standing at. The damage that happens in unguarded places isn't always dramatic. A lot of it is slow, subtle, and consistent. And by the time people notice it, the root has already gone deep. The watchman who stays on the wall prevents that. Not by being perfect. By being present.

There's also a legislative dimension to the final call that every *Shamar* watchman needs to carry. You're not just a person who prays. You're a member of the government of God. You're part of the *ecclesia*, the judicial and legislative people of God, who have been given the keys of the kingdom and the authority to bind and loose in the spirit realm. Every decree you issue from the courts of heaven has legal standing. Every contract you establish through binding and loosing is enforced by heaven. The enemy can't just ignore what you've legally established in the spirit. He has to respond to it. And a watchman who understands this doesn't just pray hoping something shifts. They legislate. They govern the atmosphere over their assigned territory with the authority of someone who knows they're standing in the right court, through the right blood, with the right evidence.

The difference in a person whose life goes up and a person whose life goes down is their ability to pray. Not just to say words. To know how to pray. Prayer is an art. It's not just emotion. It's not just volume. It's kingdom principles applied with precision and faith. The person who knows how to build their case in the courts of heaven, who knows how to activate the right principle at the right time, who knows how to stand in the gap with the authority of an ambassador and the faithfulness of a guardian, that person doesn't just survive the hard seasons. They change the outcome of those seasons for everyone in their sphere.

You were built for this. The desires that have been in your heart since you were young weren't accidents. The burden you carry for the people in your life isn't a personality trait. The way you wake up at three in the morning with a weight you can't explain isn't anxiety. It's a call. It's the *Shamar* anointing, the ancient guardian call, pressing on your spirit because God designed you to stand at this gate, in this hour, for these people. And He's been preparing you for it through every valley you've walked through, every gate you've passed through, every season of crushing that delivered you from what shouldn't have been there so you could carry what He actually designed for you.

Stay on the wall. Not because it's easy. Because there are too many souls on the line to come down. Not because you always see results. Because the wall is being built, gate by gate, prayer by prayer, decree by decree, whether you can see it or not. Not because you have it all figured out. Because the One who sent you has it all figured out, and your job is to stay in your place and trust His sovereignty over everything you can't control.

The East Gate is closer than it looks. The King is coming back. And when He does, He's looking for watchmen who stayed at their post. Who kept building when the enemy tried to discourage them. Who kept their identity when the enemy tried to slander them. Who kept their clarity when the enemy tried to confuse them. Who prayed people through the cycle even when the cycle was long. Who stood in the gap even when no one else knew they were standing there.

That's the *Shamar* anointing. That's the ancient guardian call over your family and your city. And it doesn't end until the King comes through the East Gate.

Commit, Renew, and Stay

Everything in this chapter, and everything in this book, has been building toward one moment. Not a feeling. A decision. The decision to take your place on the wall and refuse to leave it. The decision to carry the *Shamar* anointing over your family and your city with the full understanding of what it costs, what it requires, and what it accomplishes in the spirit realm. The decision to be the person God was looking for in Ezekiel 22, the one He found when He searched for someone to stand in the gap.

God's sovereignty ensures that even your failures can be redeemed through His mercy. The valley you went through didn't disqualify you. The seasons where you came off the wall didn't end your assignment. The times when discouragement won for a season didn't cancel what God wrote about you before you were born. His mercy is bigger than your history. And His call on your life is irrevocable. Romans 11:29 says the gifts and calling of God are without repentance. He doesn't take them back. He doesn't reassign them to someone else because you had a hard season. He waits. He works through the valley to deliver you from what would have corrupted the assignment. He brings you to the Dung Gate to remove what shouldn't be there. He fills you at the Fountain Gate with what you need to carry what He designed for you. And then He brings you back to the wall, better equipped than before, carrying less of the old self and more of what He actually put there.

Your final action steps are four. They're not complicated. But they require commitment. Do them in order and do them this week.

The first action step is to write a formal renewal of your watchman's vow. Not a prayer. A vow. A specific, written commitment to God that you're renewing your assignment as a *Shamar* watchman over your assigned *metron*. Write it in first person. Make it specific. Name the territory God has given you. Name the people you're assigned to guard. Name the gates you're committing to stand at. Write it by hand if you can. There's something about the physical act of writing a vow that anchors it in a way that typing doesn't. Speak it out loud when you're done. Date it. Keep it somewhere you'll see it regularly. This is your formal recommitment to your post. The enemy saw you read this book. He knows what you know now. Your vow is a legal declaration in the courts of heaven that you're not moving.

The second action step is to identify one person in your *metron* who is currently in the most critical place in the Nehemiah cycle and commit to thirty days of targeted, daily intercession specifically for that person. One person. Named. Specific. Using everything you've learned in this book. Locate them in the cycle. Identify the gate they're at. Pray the specific prayer for that gate every single day for thirty days. Build your case in the courts of heaven on their behalf. Activate a kingdom principle that corresponds to what they need. Decree their destiny out loud over them by name. Thirty days. Consistent. Specific. That's not a small commitment. But it's exactly the kind of faithfulness that moves people through gates they couldn't get through on their own.

The third action step is to establish one specific accountability structure for your watchman call. Not just a prayer partner. An accountability relationship with someone who knows your assignment, who will ask you regularly whether you're staying on the wall, who will speak truth to you when the three spirits are working against you, and who you can call when the battle gets heavy. This person should be someone under the same or a higher spiritual covering than you. Someone who carries the same kind of call. Someone who will tell you the truth even when you don't want to hear it. Reach out to that person this week. Tell them what you're committing to. Ask them to hold you accountable to it. A watchman who is accountable to someone is a watchman who is much harder to pull off the wall.

The fourth action step is to begin the practice of the East Gate prayer every morning starting tomorrow. Before you pray anything else, before your list, before your decrees, before your intercession, speak these words out loud: "Lord, I stand at my post today with the awareness that you are coming back. I pray with the urgency of a watchman who knows the time is short. Every prayer I pray today, I pray in the context of eternity. Let my intercession push the people you've given me toward readiness for your return. I am on the wall. I am not moving. Come, Lord Jesus." Thirty seconds. Every morning. It repositions everything that follows. It anchors your prayer life in the ultimate purpose of the *Shamar* call. And it keeps the East Gate alive in your spirit every single day until the King walks through it.

The wall doesn't build itself. The gates don't open on their own. The souls in your sphere won't find their way through the cycle without someone standing in the gap for them. But with a watchman who understands their authority, who knows their *metron*, who prays from the courts of heaven with legal standing through the blood of Jesus, who stays at their post through every attack the enemy sends, things move. People come home. Valleys end. Purpose is birthed. The glory cloud forms. And the King finds His people ready when He returns through the East Gate.

You are a foundational piece of God's kingdom. Even when you aren't seen. Even when no one knows you were there. Your presence on the wall is holding something together that would fall apart without you. The structure of your family's spiritual life, the atmosphere of your church, the spiritual climate of your city, all of it is being shaped by whether or not a watchman is at their post. You are that watchman. You've always been that watchman. And now you know it.

Stay on the wall.

Activation & Reflection

---

1. How do you hold the tension between God's sovereignty and your responsibility to intercede? Do you tend toward passivity or toward anxious striving?

____

____

____

____

2. Have you experienced a situation where judgment came despite your intercession? How did you process that spiritually?

____

____

____

____

3. How does understanding God's mercy within judgment shape the way you pray for nations, communities, or individuals under spiritual correction?

____

____

____

____

4. What did Moses, Abraham, and Daniel teach us about standing in the gap when judgment is imminent? Which of their postures challenges you most?

____

____

____

____

5. Write a prayer of intercession for a person, city, or nation that you believe is on the threshold of God's corrective judgment.

____

____

____

____

A Prayer of Merciful Intercession

Sovereign Lord, I stand in the gap between Your justice and Your mercy. Like Moses, I place myself in the breach and plead for grace where judgment has been deserved. I do not minimize sin, but I magnify Your covenant faithfulness. Have mercy, Lord — not because we deserve it, but because of who You are. Turn hearts back to You before the hour of correction arrives. Let mercy triumph over judgment. In Jesus' name, Amen.

CONCLUSION

The Guardian's Legacy

The Guardian\'s Legacy

You've come a long way from where this started.

When you opened this book, you may have known something was stirring in you but couldn't name it. You felt the pull to pray. You sensed things others didn't sense. You woke up at odd hours with burdens that didn't belong to you. And now you know what that is. It's not a quirk of your personality. It's not spiritual overload. It's a call. Specifically, it's the *Shamar* anointing, the ancient guardian call that God has been placing on His people since He first told Adam to keep and guard the garden.

You are more than a petitioner. You always were. But now you have the language, the understanding, and the tools to actually function in the fullness of what God designed you to carry. You're a spiritual governor. A legal advocate for the Kingdom of God. A watchman who stands between heaven and earth and refuses to move until things shift.

That's not a small thing to carry. And it's not a small thing to understand.

Every chapter in this book was building toward one reality: that the people God placed in your sphere of influence need you at your post. They need you on the wall. Not occasionally. Not when you feel spiritually strong. Consistently. Daily. With one hand building and one hand fighting, the way Nehemiah built the walls of Jerusalem while the enemy was still trying to stop him. That image isn't just a historical account. It's a picture of what your life as a *Shamar* watchman looks like in the real world, in the middle of your actual schedule, with your actual family, in your actual church, in your actual city.

You're not doing this from a monastery. You're doing it from your kitchen table, your car, your prayer closet, your workplace. Wherever God has placed you is where the wall gets built.

Think about what you now carry that you didn't carry before. You understand your *metron*, the specific territory where your prayers carry the most legal weight. You know the Nehemiah Intercession Roadmap and can locate every person in your sphere at a specific gate in the cycle, which means you can pray for them with precision instead of just praying in hope. You understand the courts of heaven and how to present your case through the blood of Jesus with evidence, with covenant ground, and with the legal authority of a member of the *ecclesia*. You know the three spirits that will come at you on the wall and you know how to name them, resist them, and stay in your place when they do. You know how to build the glory cloud through the seven Hebrew expressions of praise. You know how to guard your ear gate and wash your mind with the Word. You know how to govern the atmosphere of your home, your meetings, and your assigned territory. You understand prevenient grace and the legal covering your covenant with God has already placed over your household. And you understand the weight of the East Gate, the urgency of the hour, and the reality that the King is coming back and the people in your sphere need to be ready when He does.

That's not theory. That's a toolkit. And a watchman with a toolkit is a completely different force in the spirit than a believer who just prays and hopes.

Your importance in the body of Christ is not negotiable. The body of Christ doesn't function without watchmen. Families don't stay protected without someone standing in the gap. Churches don't stay unified without an intercessor praying through the tensions before they become public fractures. Cities don't shift without watchmen who understand territorial authority and know how to legislate heaven's agenda over their region. You are a foundational pillar. The vision of God stands firm against the storms of this age because people like you refuse to come off the wall.

Don't let the enemy convince you otherwise. He will try. He always does. He'll send Sanballat to whisper that you've been at this too long and nothing is changing. He'll send Tobiah to attack your character and make the people in your sphere doubt who you are. He'll send the Ashdodite spirit to cloud your thinking about your calling until you can't remember why you started. All three of those spirits have one goal: get you off the wall. Nehemiah never came down. And neither do you.

Step Into Your New Authority

Knowing is not the same as doing.

You can understand every concept in this book at an intellectual level and still be standing in the same place you were before you started reading. Knowledge without action is just information. And information doesn't build walls. Faithfulness does. Consistent, daily, unglamorous, nobody-sees-it faithfulness is what builds the wall. It's what pushes people through the gates of the Nehemiah cycle. It's what creates the glory cloud. It's what shifts the atmosphere over a family, a church, a city.

The time for moving from the theory of the watchtower into the reality of the wall is now. Not when you feel more ready. Not when your circumstances are more favorable. Not after you've prayed about it for another few weeks. Now. Because the people in your *metron* are at their gates right now. Some of them are stuck between the Valley Gate and the Dung Gate, sitting in the middle of everything God was trying to remove, unable to get up without someone standing in the gap for them. Some of them are right at the edge of the Water Gate, on the threshold of their divine purpose, being held back by fear while a watchman who understood their assignment could decree that fear broken in the name of Jesus and watch them walk through. Some of them aren't saved yet, being drawn by the prevenient grace that your covenant with God has already activated over your household, waiting for the right divine appointment that your prayers are helping to set up.

They need you moving. Not just knowing.

By applying the legislative prayer principles in this book, by maintaining your spiritual covering, by building your case in the courts of heaven with scripture and covenant ground and the blood of Jesus, you will see things shift. Not always on your timeline. Not always in the way you expected. But the spiritual reality is clear: the effective prayer of a righteous person accomplishes much. The word effective is the key. Effective prayer is aimed prayer. It knows what it's pushing toward and it pushes. And you now know how to aim.

Your family can be saved. Your city can shift. Your own peace can be restored to a depth you haven't experienced before, the peace that comes not from having everything figured out but from knowing that you're in your place, doing what you were designed to do, standing in the gap for the people God specifically assigned to your care. That peace is available to you. But it only comes to the watchman who is actually on the wall, not to the one who is still deciding whether to climb it.

The outcome of your life and the lives of those you love depends on your willingness to stay on the wall and refuse to negotiate with the spirits of discouragement and confusion. That's not pressure meant to burden you. It's the truth meant to anchor you. You matter in the spirit realm in ways you can't fully see yet. The wall you're building through your prayers is real. The gates you're pushing people through are real. The decrees you're issuing in the courts of heaven are legally binding. And the enemy knows it. That's why he works so hard to pull you off your post. A watchman who knows their authority and uses it consistently is one of the most dangerous forces in the kingdom of God.

Be that force.

Your Step-by-Step Blueprint for the Wall

Everything you need to live out the *Shamar* anointing is already in your hands. What follows is a clear, specific, ordered blueprint for putting it all together into a daily and weekly practice that actually functions in the real world.

Start by defining your *metron* clearly. If you haven't already done the exercise from Chapter 5, do it today. Draw your three circles on a blank piece of paper. In the innermost circle, write the names of the people in your household. In the middle circle, write the names of your close church community, your spiritual relationships, the people you have consistent meaningful contact with. In the outer circle, write your city or region. That map is your assigned territory.

Those are the people your prayers carry the most legal weight for. Look at that map every day. Pray over every name in it. That's your post. You don't abandon it.

Once your *metron* is clear, locate the people in it on the Nehemiah Intercession Roadmap. Go through each name in your inner circle and honestly identify which gate they're currently at. Are they at the Sheep Gate, not yet saved, needing the grace of God to draw them and every spirit of blindness to be broken off their mind? Are they stuck at the Valley Gate or the Dung Gate, going around the same mountain, unable to release what the valley was supposed to remove? Are they ready for the Fountain Gate, needing a fresh filling of the Holy Spirit and a fresh vision for their next season? Are they at the Water Gate, standing on the threshold of their divine purpose, needing someone to decree that fear and confusion are broken off their assignment? Locate them. Write it down. That's your prayer target. That's where you aim.

Then establish your daily practice of the seven Hebrew praises. Not all seven every day in one sitting. But across the course of your week, all seven should appear somewhere in your worship life. Begin your prayer times with *Barak*, physically kneeling and bringing your body into submission before God. Lift your hands in *Yada* and confess His sovereignty over everything in your sphere. Let *Shabach* be your weekly shout of testimony over the specific people in your *metron*. Practice *Halal* with the kind of uninhibited celebration that breaks the spirit of heaviness off your life and your home. Use *Zamar* to cultivate the spirit of prophecy through intentional musical worship, then sit in silence afterward and listen for what God wants to say about your assigned territory. Let *Tehillah* be the spontaneous song that creates a dwelling place for God's presence in your life. And weave *Todah* through your daily prayers as consistent thanksgiving for who God is and what He's already doing in the people you're standing in the gap for. These seven expressions aren't just worship tools. They're cloud-building tools. Every time you use them, you're adding to the glory cloud that forms around your life and governs the atmosphere of every space you're assigned to protect.

Move into legislative intercession every day. Not petition prayer. Decree. Build your case from the Word of God. Come before the courts of heaven through the blood of Jesus. Find the specific scripture that speaks to the specific situation you're bringing before God. Write out your formal decree in present tense. Speak it out loud. Hold it. Don't pray it once and then go back to worrying. A decree that's been issued needs to be maintained. Come back to it daily. Speak it again. Remind yourself and the spirit realm of what has been legally established. The wall is built gate by gate, prayer by prayer, decree by decree. Keep building.

Guard your ear gate with the same intentionality you bring to your intercession. What you allow through that gate shapes what you believe, how you pray, and how effectively you stand in the gap. Identify one recurring thought that the enemy has been using as a missile against your calling and find the specific scripture that directly contradicts it. Speak that scripture out loud every time the thought arrives. Don't fight the thought with more thoughts. Out-speak it. Send truth through the same gate the lie tried to enter. Do this until the frequency and intensity of that thought diminishes. It will. The Word doesn't fail.

Stay aligned with your spiritual covering. Pray for them specifically and consistently. Submit your assignment to them. Receive their impartation with an open heart rather than a critical one. Let their grace extend to cover your battles. Don't go where you haven't been sent. Don't engage in high-level spiritual warfare in territories where you have no assignment and no covering. Be invited or be sent. Those three words will protect you from more spiritual backlash than almost anything else in this book. The ambassador who moves with the backing of the government they represent is a completely different force than the rebel who moves on their own initiative. Be the ambassador.

Sweep your home regularly. Anoint your doorposts. Declare each room a zone of the glory cloud. Practice the threshold prayer every time you come home, shaking off whatever you picked up in the environments you moved through during the day. Keep the atmosphere of your home sanctuary clean and governed. Your children live in that atmosphere every day. Your marriage breathes it. Your own spiritual clarity depends on it. A watchman who governs their home well is a watchman who shows up to prayer with a clean environment to work from.

Keep the East Gate in your spirit every single morning. Before you pray anything else, speak it out loud. "Lord, I stand at my post today with the awareness that you are coming back. I pray with the urgency of a watchman who knows the time is short. Let my intercession today push the people you've given me toward readiness for your return. I am on the wall. I am not moving." Thirty seconds. Every morning. It repositions everything that follows. It anchors your prayer life in the ultimate purpose of the *Shamar* call and keeps you from drifting into a routine that's lost its urgency.

And when the three spirits come at you, because they will, name them. Don't let Sanballat make you believe your prayers aren't doing anything. Don't let Tobiah make you more concerned with your reputation than your assignment. Don't let the Ashdodite spirit cloud your thinking about who you are and what God called you to do. Name the spirit. Speak the warfare decree. Stay on the wall. Keep building. The wall is almost complete. The enemy intensifies the pressure right before the breakthrough because he knows it's coming. When the attack gets louder, don't interpret it as a sign that nothing is happening. Interpret it as a sign that something is about to.

The *Shamar* anointing over your family and your city is built in the daily choices. The choice to get up and pray when you don't feel like it. The choice to issue a decree instead of sinking into anxiety. The choice to govern your atmosphere instead of being governed by it. The choice to stay under your covering instead of going rogue with your zeal. The choice to build the glory cloud through worship instead of letting the dryness win. The choice to stay on the wall when Sanballat, Tobiah, and the Ashdodites are all talking at once.

Every one of those choices is a stone in the wall. Every one of them matters. Every one of them is being recorded in the books of heaven. And one day, when you stand at the Inspection Gate and give your account, the question will be the same one God asked Adam in the garden: where are you? Not in terms of geography. In terms of assignment. Were you at your post? Did you stay? Did you guard what I gave you? Did you keep what I placed in your care?

The answer you give that day is being written right now. One prayer at a time. One decree at a time. One gate at a time. One person at a time.

Stay on the wall.

Activation & Reflection

---

1. What has shifted most deeply in your understanding of intercession and the watchman's call since beginning this journey?

____

____

____

____

2. What legacy do you want to leave as an intercessor? Who will carry the torch because you were faithful at your post?

____

____

____

____

3. What is one truth from this book that has permanently altered the way you will pray going forward?

____

____

____

____

4. Who are the next-generation watchmen in your life that you are responsible for training, covering, and releasing?

____

____

____

____

5. Write a personal covenant between you and God — a formal commitment to take your place on the wall and not come down until the assignment is complete.

____

____

____

____

The Guardian's Covenant Prayer

Lord God, I covenant with You today to be a faithful guardian on the wall for the rest of my days. I will not be moved by discouragement, silenced by slander, or confused by the enemy's tactics. I plant my feet and declare: I will watch. I will pray. I will decree. I will not come down from my post until You release me or call me home. The legacy I leave will be one of faithfulness, fire, and fruit. Use my life, Lord, as a living altar. The watchman is on the wall. In Jesus' name, Amen.

ABOUT THE AUTHOR

Johnathan Stidham Ministries is passionate about helping individuals grow in their faith and deepen their relationship with God. The mission is to equip believers with the tools, wisdom, and guidance they need to live Spirit-filled, purpose-driven lives.

About Dr. Johnathan Stidham

Dr. Johnathan L. Stidham is a husband, father, author, and a man called by God to build up regions to experience the presence and manifested glory of God.

Dr. Stidham accepted the call to ministry at the age of 16, filled with a burning desire for the body of Christ to encounter miracles, signs, and wonders as the early church experienced. Known for his prophetic accuracy within the body of Christ as well as in governmental spheres, he has planted numerous churches and is the founder and overseer of a global ministry, **Johnathan Stidham Ministries.**

Dr. Stidham travels locally, nationally, and internationally to train and equip leaders, all while maintaining a thriving congregation at his home church, **Christ Embassy** in Nicholasville, Kentucky.

He is also a decorated veteran, having served two tours in Iraq and Afghanistan. His heart beats for the lost and for those suffering with ailments and infirmities, believing in restoration and the transformative power of a new life in Christ Jesus.

Johnathan and his wife, Tonya, are respected members of their community in Nicholasville, Kentucky, where they reside with their three beautiful children.

Our Mission

To empower believers to hear God's voice, understand His Word, and walk in His divine purpose for their lives.

Our Vision

We envision a world where every believer experiences the transformative power of God's presence, guided daily by His voice and equipped to fulfill their unique calling.

What We Do

Through teaching, discipleship, and outreach, we aim to:

- Provide practical resources that strengthen your faith journey.

- Host faith-based events and gatherings for spiritual growth and community.
- Share the love of Christ through local and global outreach programs.

Stay Connected

- **Website:** www.jsglobal.org
- **Social Media:** linktr.ee/DrJohnathan

Thank you for joining us on this journey to hear God's voice and transform your life. We look forward to walking alongside you as you grow in faith and purpose.

Blessings,

Dr. Johnathan Stidham and the Christ Embassy Team

www.ingramcontent.com/pod-product-compliance
Lightning Source LLC
LaVergne TN
LVHW010637110826
845149LV00014B/2867

9798995775300